THERAVADA BUDDHISM
IN SOUTHEAST ASIA

Theravada Buddhism in Southeast Asia

Robert C. Lester

BIP88   *Ann Arbor Paperbacks*

THE UNIVERSITY OF MICHIGAN PRESS

First edition as an Ann Arbor Paperback 1973
Copyright © by The University of Michigan 1973
All rights reserved
ISBN 0–472–57000–5 (clothbound)
ISBN 0–472–06184–4 (paperbound)
Library of Congress Catalog Card No. 71–185154
Published in the United States of America by
The University of Michigan Press and simultaneously
in Don Mills, Canada, by Longman Canada Limited
Manufactured in the United States of America

Preface

This book is intended to communicate the major features of the present-day practice of Theravada Buddhism in Southeast Asia in the perspective of scripture and history. It is my hope that it will be informative to the specialist as well as the general reader. I have chosen to survey the entire area of Theravada influence in Southeast Asia rather than comprehensively treat the Buddhism of a single country: first, because it is possible — the great majority of the peoples of Burma, Thailand, Laos, and Cambodia adhere to a single tradition, Theravada Buddhism, and have arrived at their present practice of this tradition through several centuries of interaction; second, because I desire to convey "flavor" rather than elaborate detail and the larger study lends itself to this end; third, because the distinctive practices of each of the various peoples of the Theravada area are most notable in the light of larger common patterns; and finally, because these variations within a single tradition frequently cut across national borders — e.g., the Buddhism practiced by the Shan people of Northern Burma is in many ways more akin to that practiced in Northern Thailand than to that practiced by the Burmese; the Buddhism of the Northeast Thai is more akin to that of the Lao than to that of the rest of Thailand.

Ceylonese Theravada Buddhism, except as to its historical impact on Southeast Asia, is excluded from this study. Ceylonese Buddhists played a major role in the early development of Theravada Buddhism in Southeast Asia, and the three most significant orders within the Ceylonese monastic community today honor ordination lines established from Thailand and Burma. Even so, patterns of Buddhist life in contemporary Ceylon vary so significantly from those of Southeast Asia as to demand separate treatment and constant exception from the generalizations otherwise possible. Due largely to geographical location, Ceylon has been more heavily influenced by Indian culture than has Theravada Southeast Asia and correspondingly has not been party to the long-term interaction of the peoples of mainland Southeast Asia. Having sizable Hindu and Christian minorities, Ceylon is only 64 percent Buddhist; whereas Theravada Southeast Asia is 85 to 95 percent Buddhist. Unlike the monastic orders of Southeast Asia, the monastic community in Ceylon is internally divided by caste. Those ordained to the monastic life in Ceylon are expected to commit for a lifetime; whereas in Southeast Asia the great majority who become monks remain so for only a few months or few years, leaving without stigma attached. These factors together make for significant differences between Ceylon and Theravada Southeast Asia in patterns of monastic life and monk-lay interaction.

In order to view Buddhism as it is actually lived, yet in historical perspective and in the light of the Buddhist's professed ideal, it is necessary to draw upon the insights of scholars representing several different disciplines. This is no doubt precarious — one is never certain that he is fairly applying insights taken out of the particular context in which they were first expounded. I hope that whatever the faults of this study it will at the least provide a basis for further, much-needed macrostudies of the culture of mainland Southeast Asia.

Preface

The fieldwork for this study was done under a Fulbright-Hays Faculty Fellowship. I wish to gratefully acknowledge the assistance of the members of the faculty of the Southeast Asia Studies Program at Cornell University, and the South-Southeast Asia Study Center at The American University, Washington, D.C. I wish to thank the Pali Text Society for permission to reprint excerpts from *Dialogues of the Buddha* and *Book of the Gradual Sayings*. My special thanks to Mr. John Thomson, friend and former colleague, and to my wife, Donna, typist, consultant, and critic.

Contents

Introduction

Buddhism as philosophy and as a meditative discipline has been known and appreciated in the Western world for some time. Buddhism as the way of life of a people, an all-encompassing, multileveled life-style, the instrument of a people's identity and cultural continuity, is not so well known. This is regrettable considering the present worldwide interest and involvement in mainland Southeast Asia, where the great majority of the peoples indeed adhere to Buddhism as a way of life — here the whole drama of human existence is played out in the framework of Buddhist values.

In recent years the peoples of Burma, Thailand, Laos, and Cambodia have appealed to Buddhism as the ground of nationalism and not without justification. There is a profound sense in which to be Burmese, Thai, Lao, or Cambodian is to be Buddhist. In these Theravada[1] Buddhist countries Buddhist values inform and inspire basic social, economic, and political patterns of life for the individual, family, village, and nation. Theravada Buddhism is the established religion of the kingdoms of Thailand, Laos, and Cambodia and as such receives extensive patronage and guidance from king and government. In Burma Buddhist revival has proceeded hand in hand with Burmese nationalism. Buddhism, established under U Nu (1961) only to be disestablished a

1

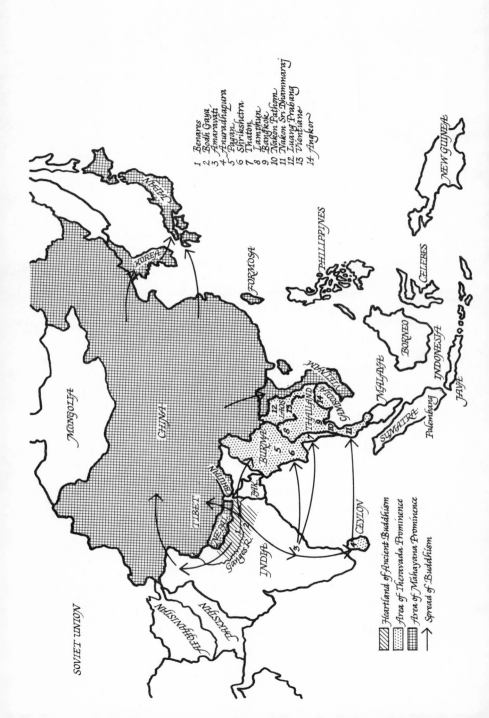

1 Benares
2 Bodh Gaya
3 Amaravati
4 Anuradhapura
5 Pagan
6 Shrikshetra
7 Thaton
8 Lamphun
9 Bangkok
10 Nakon Pathom
11 Nakon Sri Dhammaraj
12 Luang Prabang
13 Vientiane
14 Angkor

Heartland of Ancient Buddhism
Area of Theravada Prominence
Area of Mahayana Prominence
→ Spread of Buddhism

short time later under Ne Win, still enjoys substantial recognition and support from government.

We will have great difficulty in understanding Buddhism as practiced in Southeast Asia unless we attempt to take it on its own terms. If we think about Buddhism in general terms as a 'religion', rather than as a particular way of life of a particular people in a time, place, and circumstances, we inevitably apply to it certain Western stereotypes, a Western cultural bias, concerning religion. We may, for instance, think about religion as having to do with 'God' when Theravada Buddhism does not recognize 'God'. We may think about religion as a realm of human experience and institutions distinct from politics, commerce, and general social patterns when neither the Buddhist ideal embodied in scripture and tradition nor the practicing Buddhist recognizes such distinctions. The religious-secular dichotomy applied so extensively in Western thought is inappropriate to the Buddhist way in Southeast Asia. The Theravada Buddhist (aside from a small minority of somewhat Westernized urban Southeast Asians) thinks of his whole way of life as Buddhist — his individual, family, village, and national cultural identity is established with reference to Buddhist values. Western notions of 'Church' and 'State' are not appropriately applied to a Buddhist frame of reference — even to use the word 'Church', no matter how well defined, is to occasion an illegitimate transference in the Western mind from a Judeo-Christian heritage to Buddhism. We must recognize not only that the Theravada countries of Southeast Asia own a long-standing tradition of close association and cooperation between government and expressly Buddhist organizations and leadership but that government itself rightly viewed is a Buddhist institution. Even the 'sacred-profane' dichotomy has limited applicability in Buddhist cultures. To the Buddhist there is something special about a Buddha-image, a monastery, and a Buddhist monk, but special in degree rather than kind. Inasmuch as all life is understood in terms of Buddhist values, everything is 'sacred'. Theravada Buddhists speak of their way of life as the Buddha-Sasana — the 'Buddha-context'[2] within which all kinds and conditions of men (and all other sentient beings) pursue the Buddha-enlightenment according to their individual capacity and circumstances — some take up the way of the monk, others follow the lay way; all are on the path of the Buddha. There are here no 'religious' persons as opposed to 'nonreligious' persons; there are only those who are as individuals at one stage or another of self-discipline along the same path.

Due in part to cultural bias, but also to a misreading of Buddhist texts and a failure to examine the Buddhism of twentieth-century practice as well as the Buddhism of the scriptures, most Western studies of Theravada Buddhism promote a wrong image. If our intent is to understand living Buddhism in Southeast Asia, we must not only examine Buddhist texts through the eyes of practicing Buddhists, but also become familiar with present-day Buddhist patterns of life. An attempt to understand twentieth-century Buddhism on the basis of ancient scripture alone is comparable to attempting to comprehend twentieth-century American Protestant Christianity simply by studying the Bible. Western historical-textual studies consistently present Theravada Buddhism as a rigorously monastic, ascetic, and meditative discipline pursuant of liberation from the sorrow and suffering of human existence.[3] This view not only excludes the nonmonk, but also distorts the way of the monk by examining it apart from the way of the layman. Further, characterization of Theravada Buddhism as a way of monks has moved some observers of Buddhist Southeast Asia to conclude that the mass of the people are not Buddhist at all but animists.[4] This is a rather gross distortion of scriptural Buddhism as well as practiced Buddhism.

Recent sociological and anthropological studies of Southeast Asian Buddhist peoples provide needed new insight on the practice of Theravada Buddhism and encouragement to take a fresh look at Buddhist texts. Village studies inventorying and analyzing the various symbols, rituals, and patterns of life operative among Buddhist peoples reveal the depth and breadth of the sphere of Buddhist influence, the social dynamics of life lived in accordance with Buddhist values, and the nature of the inspiration which Buddhist peoples derive from ancient texts. The careful, empathic analysis of patterns of life can give insights into living Buddhism which can never be provided by historical-textual studies. This is not, however, to dismiss historical and literary studies as irrelevant to our subject. The social scientist is no less subject to cultural bias, inference from the standpoint of alien values, than is the historian or textual analyst. And more importantly, social studies frequently lack 'depth perception'. The social scientist may come at his subject without sufficient historical and theoretical (doctrinal, etc.) perspective and thereby elaborately describe what he does not really understand. We must work for a balanced view of contemporary Southeast Asian Buddhism receiving insight from various quarters.[5] Social studies tell us something of the way people believe and act; historical-textual studies tell us something of why they believe and act the way they do. One must continually go back and forth from the surface phenomena to history and tradition. This is necessary not only with respect to Southeast Asian Buddhism generally but also with respect to the Buddhism of each of the different peoples of the area. The Burmese, Thai, Lao, and Cambodians adhere to the same Theravada tradition and some generalization is possible. Yet, each people has its own particular history, and significant variations thereby occur.

Given the insights of the historian, textual analyst, and social scientist, we gain a view of Southeast Asian Theravada Buddhism rather different from the presently prevailing image. One who becomes a monk does indeed renounce the world but in and through this very renunciation he becomes a 'saving' instrument *for* the world, a mediator of the Buddha-power. At one and the same time he is renounced and yet thoroughly involved in the society around him — through withdrawal he achieves among his people a status without

5

equal; he is seen as the embodiment of the ideal life-style. He cultivates, carries, and radiates the wisdom, compassion, and power of the Buddha to all beings. He may serve his community as preacher of the Buddha-word; teacher of youth; healer of the sick; respected counselor of all kinds and conditions of men; hallower of the great occasions of family, village, and national life; exorcist of the malevolent spirit forces which play upon worldly human existence; social welfare worker; and political integrator — key agent in social, economic, and political change. This is nothing essentially new to Theravada Buddhism. From time to time throughout a long history the specific way in which the monk has exercised his status has changed, and it is changing with considerable significance in our time; but he has always enjoyed such status, he has always existed for the world. This was true of the Buddha himself who, respected by kings, settled quarrels between great powers, healed the sick, and counseled on the whole gamut of worldly affairs.

The monastery, seemingly shut off from the world by its compound walls, is in fact the very hub of village life. It may serve not only as a place of residence, study, and meditation for the monk, but also as school, social center, medical dispensary, and counseling center, home for the aged and destitute, news and information center, and social work and welfare agency for the larger society.

Of course, monk and monastery neither hold this status nor function in such roles without the laity. The monk may be closest to the top of the mountain, the end of the path, but he exists and functions as part of a mutually supportive universe of beings. The layman as well as the monk is on the path of the Buddha. Scripture, tradition, and contemporary practice recognize the various kinds and conditions of men — indeed, all living beings, spirits, gods, animals, and so forth — as at different levels of self-discipline on the road to enlightenment. Each individual being 'plugs in' to the Buddha-power, wisdom, and compassion according to his present capability (merit-status) conditioned by his past. But more,

6

each being enhances his own status through service to other beings — *this is the peculiar dynamic of the Theravada way of life*, that each man's fate is in his own hands, yet advancement toward the ideal depends upon meritorious interaction with other beings. The Buddhist speaks of self-discipline status as merit-status. The monk is a 'merit-field' for the layman, the layman a 'merit-maker'. The layman is a 'merit-field' for the monk, the monk a 'merit-maker'. The monk, uncompromised by the world, most truly exemplifies the ideal — the layman recognizing, honoring, and serving the monk (and thus the ideal) enhances his merit-status; that is, he cultivates and manifests a certain self-discipline, a quality of life characterized by 'giving'. But this is mutual, not one way — the monk in providing the layman with the opportunity to give enhances his own merit-status by cultivating and manifesting humility and compassion. Stated in practical terms from the two different angles, the monk voluntarily gives up the joys of life in the world toward the development of high character, wisdom, and compassion — the layman moved by such an example of purity responds by feeding, clothing, and housing the monk, calling on his aid, and in every way honoring him; the layman grapples with the exigencies of life in the world in order to support the monk — the monk in gratitude responds by preaching, teaching, counseling, and blessing. Merit-interaction takes place in numerous different ways and at various levels in the society. King and government make merit and give merit for a nation — at this level merit-action may be a key means of national integration and unity. When we have considered the various patterns of merit-activity, we shall see how an entire social system operates with reference to Buddhist values.

Given this kind of society the layman must be considered as much a Buddhist as the monk. Further, it must be noted that in the Theravada societies of Southeast Asia the line between monk and layman is not a hard one — the male member of the society may move between the status and role of monk and of layman with relative ease. Ideally, every male should at some time in his life, preferably when coming of age and just before marriage, take up the way of the monk for at least a short time. One of the greatest sources of merit for all involved is an ordination to the monkhood. For the purpose of discussion we must label and categorize Buddhists and their activities, but we must bear in mind that we are dealing with a living fluid entity, many-faced and moving, never fully comprehended by the concepts of man's mind.

It is readily evident that Buddhist values signally condition patterns of life in Theravada Southeast Asia. It is also quite evident that today there are strong forces at work in Southeast Asia, pressures for rapid change toward Westernization and so-called modernization, and foreign agencies, which do not necessarily recognize or respect Buddhist values or those who most clearly exemplify these values, the Buddhist monks. Throughout our study we shall try to take cognizance of these forces and the ways in which Buddhism has responded to them, the potential in Buddhist values and institutions for permitting, supporting, and/or motivating certain kinds of social, economic, and political change. There are many concerned with development in the underdeveloped nations of Southeast Asia, particularly non-Asians, who consider the monk and Buddhist values antithetic to modernization. Of course they make this judgment without knowledge of the Buddhist tradition and in light of modernization ideals based on non-Asian values. Whether or not Buddhist values foster realization of modernization ideals depends very much on the value-framework assumed, the ideals sought after. We must ask: What kind of a society and world does Southeast Asian Buddhism intend? What are the forces at work in the context of Buddhist values? What ideals do they and can they foster? Is it necessarily the case that a more satisfactory life for Buddhist peoples must be built on the basis of Western models?

PART I
The Ideal in Scripture and Tradition

I

The Buddha

T HERAVADA BUDDHISTS affirm the ideal inspiring their way of life in the frequently recited "threefold refuge" (*ti-sarana*):

Buddham saranam gacchami — "I go to the Buddha as refuge."

Dhammam saranam gacchami — "I go to the Dhamma as refuge."

Sangham saranam gacchami — "I go to the Sangha as refuge."

. . . The elect disciple is in this world possessed of faith in the Buddha — believing the Blessed One to be the Holy One, the Fully-enlightened One, Wise, Upright, Happy, World-knowing, Supreme, the Bridler of men's wayward hearts, the Teacher of gods and men, the Blessed Buddha. . . . He (the disciple) is possessed of faith in the Truth [Dhamma] — believing the truth to have been proclaimed by the Blessed One, of advantage in this world, passing not away, welcoming all, leading to salvation, and to be attained to by the wise, each one for himself. . . . He (the disciple) is possessed of faith in the Order [Sangha] — believing the multitude of the disciples of the Blessed One who are walking in the four

11

stages of the noble eightfold path, the righteous, the upright, the just, the law-abiding — believing this church
of the Buddha to be worthy of honour, of hospitality, of
gifts, and of reverence; to be the supreme sowing
ground of merit for the world; to be possessed of the
virtues beloved by the good, virtues unbroken, intact,
unspotted, unblemished, virtues which make men truly
free, virtues which are praised by the wise, are untar-
nished by the desire of future life or by the belief in the
efficacy of outward acts, and are conducive to high and
holy thought.[1]

The authoritative definition of Buddha, Dhamma, and
Sangha is embodied in the *Tipiṭaka* ("Three Baskets"), composed of the Sutta (discourses), Vinaya (a collection of rules
and regulations for the monastic life), and Abhidhamma (a
collection of elaborate classifications and expositions on the
teachings of the Buddha).[2] The entire canon is attributed to
the Buddha and his earliest disciples. According to tradition[3]
it was carried orally by a particular line of monks until finally
committed to written form in the Pali language in Ceylon
in the first century B.C.[4] While Theravada Buddhists recognize that their tradition is only one of several inspired by the
Buddha, they maintain that it embodies the most authentic
record of the life and teachings of the great sage — thus, the
name Thera-vada, "The Way of the Elders." Extensive commentaries (*atthakatha*), in both Pali and Singhalese, have
been written on most of the *Tipiṭaka* and are relied upon, in
effect, as part of the canon itself. Among these the most popular is the *Jātakaṭṭhakathā* or "Birth-Stories Commentary"
which embodies the stories of the Buddha's former lives re-
ferred to only briefly in the canon. Several noncanonical
works are given special authority in the Theravada tradition:
the *Milindapañha* ("The Questions of Milinda"), a discussion of the teachings of the Buddha between a Greek king
and a Buddhist monk written around the second century
A.D.; the *Visuddhimagga* ("The Path of Purification"), a sys-

tematic presentation of the Buddha's path to Nibbana ("cessation of desire") (Sanskrit: Nirvana) attributed to one Buddhaghosa (ca. 400 A.D.);[5] and the Ceylonese chronicles, the *Dīpavaṃsa* ("The Island Chronicle") and the *Mahā-vaṃsa* ("The Great Chronicle"), relating the history of Buddhism (and Ceylon) down to the fifth century A.D.

The Buddha

Know, Vasettha, that (from time to time) a Tathagata ["Enlightened One"] is born into the world, an Arahat, a fully awakened one, abounding in wisdom and goodness, happy, with knowledge of the worlds, unsurpassed as a guide to mortals willing to be led, a teacher of gods and men, a Blessed One, a Buddha. He, by himself, thoroughly understands, and sees, as it were, face to face this universe — including the worlds above with the gods, the Maras ["Evil Ones"], and the Brahmas; and the world below with its Samanas and Brahmans, its princes and peoples; — and he then makes his knowledge known to others. The truth doth he proclaim both in the letter and in the spirit, lovely in its origin, lovely in its progress, lovely in its consummation: the higher life doth he make known, in all its purity and in all its perfectness.[6]

Looking at Buddhism from the outside, one would suppose that it began with Siddhattha Gotama, the sage of the Sakya clan (Sakyamuni), born 563 B.C., whose followers considered him the Buddha, the Enlightened One. However, for Theravada Buddhists it began "a hundred thousand cycles vast and four immensities ago"[7] when the Brahman Sumedha, having come upon the Buddha Dipamkara, vowed he also would become a Buddha:

> Come now! I'll search that I may find
> Conditions which a Buddha make —

Above, below, to all ten points,
Where'er conditions hold their sway.[8]

Life after life Sumedha pursued the Ten Perfections.[9] As a wise hare he gave himself for food to a brahman; as a wealthy prince (Vessantara) he gave all that he had (even his wife and children) to whomever asked — in these instances showing his perfection in almsgiving; as a king-elephant (Chaddanta) pierced by a poison arrow, he showed no ill will toward the hunter, cut off his own tusks while dying, and sent them to the wicked queen who employed the hunter; and later, as a great snake (Sankapala), he submitted to being pierced with sharp stakes, cut with knives, and dragged along the ground, pulled by a rope through his nose, thus attaining perfection in keeping the precepts. Having achieved the perfections, the Future Buddha was reborn in the Tusita heaven.[10] A "Buddha-Uproar" occurred, guardian angels proclaimed that a Buddha was about to be born in the world, and the gods of all the ten thousand worlds came together and addressed the Future Buddha:

> Sir, it was not to acquire the glory of a Sakka [King of the gods], or of a Mara [the Evil One], or of a Brahma [Creator-god — brings manyness out of oneness], or of a Universal Monarch, that you fulfilled the Ten Perfections; but it was to gain omniscience in order to save the world, that you fulfilled them. Sir, the time and fit season for your Buddhaship has now arrived.[11]

On the earth, in the city of Kapalivatthu, Queen Maha-maya, in a dream, is carried up into the Himalayas, bathed, and laid out on a couch in a golden mansion on a silver hill.

> Now the Future Buddha had become a superb white elephant, and was wandering about at no great distance, on Gold Hill. Descending thence, he ascended Silver Hill, and approaching from the north, he plucked a white lotus with his silvery trunk, and trumpeting loudly, went into the golden mansion. And three times

he walked round his mother's couch, with his right side towards it, and striking her on her right side, he seemed to enter her womb. Thus the conception took place in the Midsummer Festival.[12]

At that moment:

> . . . The constituent elements of the ten thousand world-systems at the same instant quaked and trembled and were shaken violently. The Thirty-two Good Omens[13] also were made manifest. In the ten thousand world-systems an immeasurable light appeared. The blind received their sight, as if from very longing to behold this his glory. The deaf heard the noise. The dumb spake one with another. The crooked became straight. The lame walked. All prisoners were freed from their bonds and chains. In each hell the fire was extinguished.[14]

Nearing the end of her pregnancy, Queen Maha-maya desires to visit her family. Enroute to her native village, she stops at a grove of sal trees blooming out of season and there, "standing up grasping a branch," gives birth to the Future Buddha. The child emerges from her side "unsmeared by any impurity" and is received on a golden net held by Maha-brahma angels. Immediately thereupon, the Future Buddha stands upright on the earth and taking seven strides forward shouts: "The chief am I in all the world."[15]

Theravada Buddhists, unlike most other Buddhists and adherents of other Indian traditions, emphasize the historicity of the Buddha — the Buddha is not a God, in his essential being transcendent of man, not to be worshipped but followed as Sumedha followed Dipamkara; he is not the only Buddha — twenty-four preceded him and one, Metteyya, is yet to come. Yet, the Buddha Sakyamuni is the Perfected One, a Superman (*mahapurisa*), the Buddha for this age, whose final birth is virgin and occasions a disturbance and rejoicing of cosmic proportions. The stories of the former births of the Buddha (Jatakas — "Lives") are as important to the Buddhist, especially the layman, as those which relate the life and teachings of the Sakya sage. These stories reveal not only the power of the Future Buddha's self-discipline, but also the nature and activities of the multitude of beings (gods, goddesses, demons, etc.) which inhabit the multi-leveled cosmos,[16] and the results of man's good and bad deeds. The main collection of Jatakas includes 550 stories, and many additions have been made by the various peoples of Ceylon and Southeast Asia on the basis of local custom and folklore. Scholarly study leaves no doubt as to the actual existence of the sage of the Sakya clan, known as Siddhattha Gotama and born somewhere in what is now Nepal about 563 B.C., but very little can be said with certainty concerning his early life. Theravada scripture and tradition assign a birth date of 624 B.C.[17] and say Gotama was born to King Suddhodana and Queen Maha-maya at Lumbini, near Rum-mindei, Nepal. King Asoka erected a pillar at this spot, third century B.C.

To return to the scriptural account, shortly after the birth, brahmans brought to the court viewed the auspicious marks[18] on the child's body and predicted:

> If a man possessing such marks and characteristics con-
> tinue in the household life, he becomes a Universal
> Monarch; if he retire from the world, he becomes a
> Buddha.[19]

At this, King Suddhodana set out to shelter Prince Siddhat-tha from experiences which might lead him to renounce the world, showering him with all the comforts of the worldly life (three castles, forty thousand dancing girls, etc.). Go-tama married and had one child, Rahula, the name meaning "fetter." The gods, however, desiring Gotama to become a Buddha, intervened and showed the young prince four signs:

> And Gotama saw, as he was driving to the park, a sick
> man, suffering and very ill, fallen and weltering in his
> own water, by some being lifted up, by others being

dressed. Seeing this, Gotama asked: "That man, good charioteer, what has he done that his eyes are not like other's eyes, nor his voice like the voice of other men?"

"He is what is called ill, my lord."

"But what is meant by ill?"

"It means, my lord, that he will hardly recover from his illness."

"But am I too, then, good charioteer, subject to fall ill; have I not got out of reach of illness?"

"You, my lord, and we too, we all are subject to fall ill; we have not got beyond the reach of illness."

"Why then, good charioteer, enough of the park for today. Drive me back hence to my rooms." . . . And he, going to his rooms, sat brooding sorrowful depressed, thinking: Shame then verily be upon this thing called birth, since to one born decay shows itself like that, disease shows itself like that.[20]

Again, Gotama sees an aged cripple and on another occasion, a funeral procession, and, each time there follows the dialogue and depressed reflection. Finally, Gotama views the serene, wandering recluse, head shaven and wearing a yellow robe. The legend of the four signs foreshadows not only Gotama's renunciation of the world at age twenty-nine, but the terms in which he would articulate his enlightenment.

The Great Renunciation takes place inevitably, under the force of Gotama's own past lives and the urgency of the entire cosmos, groaning in its suffering and yearning for Nibbana. Kanthaka, Gotama's horse, and Channa, his servant, had been reborn in their present forms in order to serve the lord in this hour. The gate to the city, made especially heavy by King Suddhodana lest his son attempt to leave, is opened by a spirit inhabiting it. Then, came Mara ("Death"), the Evil One, the personification of sense-pleasure (of everything sensuous), to tempt Gotama and deter him from the conquest of suffering and rebirth. Gotama wanders the Ganges River basin near Benares, seeking out several of the many renowned teachers who have renounced the world, meditated, and taught in the forests. After six years and having followed and found wanting many teachings including that of extreme asceticism which brought him near death, he determines to find his own way to enlightenment. Leaving his friends, he takes up meditation beneath a great banyan tree beside the River Neranjara. The aura of his body illumines the surrounding area, giving it a golden glow, such that a young girl, Sujata, thinking Gotama is the spirit of the tree, makes an offering to him. The golden rice bowl, left by Sujata and thrown on the water by Gotama, floats upstream, then sinks to the palace of the black snake-king clashing against the dishes of three former Buddhas; and Mara prepares for his final onslaught.

> As, purged of self by struggles stern, I sat
> in Reverie beside Neranjara,
> resolved to win by insight perfect peace,
> came Mara, breathing words of ruth, to say
> how lean and ill I looked, how nigh to death.
> Death owns (said he) a thousand parts of thee,
> and life can claim but one. Hold fast to life!
> Life's best; for living, thou'lt store merit up.[21]

Mara sends plague after plague upon Gotama — earthquake, whirlwind, rain, rocks, weapons, live coals, hot ashes, sand, mud, and darkness, each promptly dissipated by the force of Gotama's discipline and perfection; the showers of rocks, coals, and so forth fall at his feet as bouquets of flowers. Then Mara said:

> "Siddhattha, arise from this seat! It does not belong to you, but to me."
> When the Great Being heard this he said, — "Mara, you have not fulfilled the Ten Perfections in any of their three grades; nor have you made the five great donations; nor have you striven for knowledge, nor for the

welfare of the world, nor for enlightenment. This seat does not belong to you, but to me."[22]

Mara, enraged, hurls his mighty discus but it too is transformed into flowers providing a canopy above Gotama's head. In a final confrontation, Mara demands of Gotama: "Who is your witness to having achieved the perfections?"

> And drawing forth his right hand from beneath his priestly robe, he stretched it out towards the mighty earth, and said, "Are you witness, or are you not, to my having given a great seven-hundred-fold donation in my Vessantara existence?" And the mighty earth thundered, "I bear you witness!" with a hundred, a thousand, a hundred thousand roars, as if to overwhelm the army of Mara.[23]

Mara and his host are dispatched and the ten thousand worlds rejoice — "The victory now hath this illustrious Buddha won!"[24] Having overcome the *asavas*[25] — sensual desire, desire for existence, wrong views, and ignorance — Gotama is the Fully Awakened One, the Enlightened One, the Buddha.

After several weeks in the area of the enlightenment tree (Bodhi tree) attended by the gods,[26] Gotama ponders whether or not to teach others the truth he has realized:

> With great pains have I acquired it. Enough! Why should I now proclaim it? This doctrine will not be easy to understand to beings that are lost in lust and hatred. Given to lust, surrounded with thick darkness, they will not see what is repugnant (to their minds), abstruse, profound, difficult to perceive, and subtle.[27]

With this, the great god, Brahma, appears and with difficulty convinces Buddha that some beings will hear and heed his word. "Full of compassion towards sentient beings . . ."

Buddha goes to a deer park near Benares. Here, to former
companions he preaches his first sermon, setting in motion
the wheel of the Dhamma (Teaching). This is the beginning
of forty-five years of wandering, preaching, teaching, and
compassionate service to all kinds and conditions of men in
Northeast India.

His serene power, the "magic" of his personality are
always in evidence. In the early years following enlightenment, he gains such a following of the young and old, the
high and the lowly, that the Magadhans murmur against
him:

> The Samana Gotama causes fathers to beget no sons;
> the Samana Gotama causes wives to become widows;
> the Samana Gotama causes families to become extinct.[28]

His presence and word quickly allay their anger. A buddha
is omniscient and possesses magical power — on the occasion
of the enlistment of the ascetic Kassapa, Gotama performs
3,500 miracles. Returning to his native place, Kapalivatthu,
he performs the "miracle of the pairs," rising in the air,
flames shooting from his head and water from his feet, then
flames from one side and water from the other.[29] On another
occasion he overwhelms rival teachers by creating a road in
the sky and preaching as he walked on it. He ministers to all
kinds and conditions of men, gauging his words to the peculiar problem and capacity of each. He counsels and enlists
the support of Bimbasara, king of Magadha; he dines with
and receives a gift of a pleasure garden for his sojourn from
the prostitute, Ambapali;[30] he settles a quarrel between the
Sakyas and the Koliyas over water rights, pointing out that
men (who might be killed in battle) are of greater value
than water on earth;[31] he cleanses the sores of Tissa who is
dying of a skin disease so offensive no one else will touch
him;[32] he wondrously changes the life of Angulimala, a
notorious bandit.[33]

In spite of his compassion, he is not without enemies —
rival teachers engage a woman to feign pregnancy accusing

the Buddha of having relations with her; Devadatta and Suppabuddha, brother and father of Gotama's wife, Yasodara, are lifelong opponents of the Buddha. Devadatta, having joined the Buddha's following, attempts to gain control of the group, displacing Gotama; failing in this he encourages King Ajatasatthu to hire assassins. After the latter fails and the assassins become Buddha's followers, Devadatta himself tries to kill Gotama by hurling a rock toward him and finally by releasing a wild, intoxicated elephant in his path — the elephant is quickly subdued by the Buddha's word and kneeling recites the precepts.

Anticipating death, the Buddha retires to a secluded spot near Kusinagara and gives his final instructions to his constant companion, Ananda:

> What, then, Ananda? Does the order expect that of me? I have preached the truth without making any distinction between exoteric and esoteric doctrine: for in respect of the truths, Ananda, the Tathagata has no such thing as the closed fist of a teacher, who keeps some things back. Surely, Ananda, should there be any one who harbours the thought, "It is I who will lead the brotherhood," or, "The order is dependent upon me," it is he who should lay down instructions in any matter concerning the order. Now the Tathagata, Ananda, thinks not that it is he who should lead the brotherhood, or that the order is dependent upon him. Why then should he leave instructions in any matter concerning the order? . . . Therefore, O Ananda, be ye lamps unto yourselves. Be ye a refuge to yourselves. Betake yourselves to no external refuge. Hold fast to the truth as a lamp. Hold fast as a refuge to the truth. Look not for refuge to any one besides yourselves.[34]

On the day of the great decease, the Buddha lying on his side was surrounded by all the gods and goddesses of the world-systems weeping and wailing; Ananda, too, was sick at heart. But the Buddha points out that his death is inevitable in accordance with his own teachings, summed up in his last words:

> Decay is inherent in all component things!
> Work out your salvation with diligence![35]

There is earthquake and thunder at the moment of death; weeping and lamentation among gods and men. In accordance with the previously given instructions of the Buddha, the body is wrapped and cremated, and the remains, divided between eight claimants, are enshrined in memorial mounds (*stupas*) in various parts of the subcontinent.

II

The Dhamma

Be not at a loss what to think in this matter, and be
not greatly confused. Profound, O Vaccha, is this
doctrine, recondite, and difficult of comprehension,
good, excellent, and not to be reached by mere rea-
soning, subtile, and intelligible only to the wise . . .[1]

THE DHAMMA is what the Buddha taught through his life
and his word. It is not simply a system of ideas to be grasped
intellectually, but a path to be taken up, a way of going, a
way of moving in thought, feeling, word, and deed. The
'truths' discussed below were not intended by the Buddha as
definitive statements about the nature of reality, but as direc-
tives toward self-discipline in thinking, speaking, and acting,
as instruments of meditation. Reasoned propositions are of
value only as they are part of a total discipline of body, feeling, and mind.

The Buddha addresses life as physician rather than as
metaphysician — diagnosing the case of human existence and
prescribing the cure strictly in terms of what is given in
sense-experience. On occasion he is asked by a would-be disciple whether the world is finite or eternal, whether the soul
and the body are identical or different, whether the saint

exists after death. The Buddha replies in a parable, likening
the questioner to a man wounded with a poison arrow, demanding to know who shot the arrow — his caste, village,
color of skin, height, and so forth — before he will have his
wound attended to. Such questions are irrelevant to the one
thing needful — the healing of the wound — and before they
can be answered, if indeed they can ever be given final
answers, the man will die.[2]

> . . . The theory that the world is eternal [or that it is
> noneternal] is a jungle, a wilderness, a puppet-show, a
> writhing, and a fetter, and is coupled with misery, ruin,
> despair, and agony, and does not tend to aversion, ab-
> sence of passion, cessation, quiescence, knowledge, su-
> preme wisdom, and Nirvana.[3]

Further, the truth (validity) of the Buddha's Dhamma
must be realized by each man for himself—as in the *Kalama
Sutta*. The Kalamas who were inhabitants of Kesaputta, sitting on one side, said to the Blessed One:

> There are some monks and brahmins, venerable sir,
> who . . . illustrate and illuminate only their own doc-
> trines; the doctrines of others they despise, revile, and
> pull to pieces. Some other monks and brahmins too, . . .
> illustrate and illuminate only their own doctrines; the
> doctrines of others they despise. . . . Venerable sir, there
> is doubt, there is uncertainty, in us concerning them,
> "Which of these reverend monks and brahmins spoke
> the truth and falsehood?"

On this occasion the Buddha replied:

> It is proper for you, Kalamas, to doubt, to be uncertain.
> . . . Do not go upon what has been acquired by repeated
> hearing; nor upon tradition; nor upon rumour; nor upon
> what is in a scripture; nor upon surmise; nor upon an
> axiom; nor upon specious reasoning; nor upon a bias

towards a notion that has been pondered over; nor upon another's seeming ability; nor upon the consideration, "The monk is our teacher." Kalamas, when you yourselves know: "These things are bad; these things are blamable; these things are censured by the wise; undertaken and observed, these things lead to harm and ill," abandon them. . . . when you yourselves know: "These things are good; these things are not blamable; these things are praised by the wise; undertaken and observed, these things lead to benefit and happiness," enter on and abide in them.[4]

Theravada Buddhists find the essence of the Dhamma in the first sermon of the Buddha entitled, "Setting in Motion of the Wheel of the Dhamma."[5] Herein the Buddha teaches in terms of the Four Noble Truths:

1. The truth of Dukkha
2. The truth of the arising of Dukkha
3. The truth of the cessation of Dukkha
4. The truth of the path which leads to the cessation of Dukkha

The First Noble Truth intends to describe or diagnose the human situation — in general, human existence is unsatisfactory (*dukkha*), unsatisfying, anxiety-ridden, subject to suffering:

This is the noble truth of dukkha: birth is dukkha; decay and old age is dukkha; disease is dukkha; death is dukkha; association with what is unpleasant is dukkha; separation from what is pleasant is dukkha; failure to obtain what one wants is dukkha; briefly stated, the five groups of physical and mental processes that make up the individual, are due to grasping, and are the objects of grasping, these five groups of grasping are dukkha.[6]

The teaching begins with the recognition of the constant change or process of the human experience. The Legend of the Four Signs[7] reveals in simple form the realization of the Buddha-to-be that all beings and things are transitory (*anicca*) — all beings born must grow old, grow ill, and die. All that arises also decays — no thing, idea, state of being or mind endures. In particular, man is a 'becoming' rather than a 'being', a sequence of events rather than a conscious, permanent self — a mind, body, and selfhood ('I-ness') which consist of passing moments. Man is without *atta* ("soul") — not that he has no self, no continuity of self-reference, no individuality; but that there is no permanence about that which he perceives to be self, there is no unchanging essence underlying his becoming. The phenomena which is individual man is a constantly changing conglomerate of moments of materiality, sensations, perceptions, mental formations, and consciousnesses. The aggregate of matter or moments of materiality is the gross physical body, gross form, together with the six sense organs (organs of sight, sound, touch, taste, smell, and the mind). The aggregate of sensations is the physiological processes resulting from the contact of matter with matter, sense organs with objects of sense. The aggregate of perceptions is the mental discriminations born of sensations, the recognition of objects. The aggregate of consciousness is composed of moments of awareness. The aggregate of mental formations is composed of volitions to action (Pali: *kamma;* Sanskrit: *karma*) or the net cumulative result of past conditioning. As the arising and decaying moments of matter, sensations, perceptions, and consciousnesses interact they create a residue or energy reservoir termed mental formations which condition or occasion the continued arising and decaying of the other four aggregates. That is, the conglomerate of matter, sensations, perceptions, and consciousnesses is self-perpetuating. This is the Buddha's explanation of the law of Kamma (Karma) or the law of action: activities of thought, feeling, word, and deed occasion an accumulation of volitions to further action which result in future thoughts, feelings, words, and deeds. Thus, we are to understand that the makeup (form, etc.) and experience of the individual at any particular moment is the result of past action by that individual, and what one will be at any future moment is being conditioned by action ongoing at present. The transition from one form to another which the Hindu terms transmigration, the Buddha preferred to call 'rebirth' — as one moment is sufficient to the next, nothing 'crosses over' — the old occasions the new and in the arising of the new the old disappears. The 'I-ness' or selfhood of man, perceived as unchanging — his sense of individual being in time, having experiences — is an unwarranted extension or assumption from experience to experiencer, from knowledge to knower, thought to thinker. To appeal to the analogy presented by the monk Nagasena in the *Milindapañha*, 'I-ness' has no more (or less) existence than 'chariot' which has no being apart from the changing moments of which it is composed (wheels, axle, carriage body, banner staff, etc.). Self or soul disappears in the analysis of the moments which make it up or occasion the illusion of permanence.

> Even as the word of "chariot" means
> That members join to frame a whole;
> So when the Groups [the aggregates of matter,
>   sensation, perception, etc.] appear to view,
> We use the phrase, "A living being."[8]

Just as the word "chariot" is but a mode of expression for axles, wheels, chariot-body, pole, and other constituent members, placed in a certain relation to each other, but when we come to examine the members one by one, we discover that in the absolute sense there is no chariot; . . . in exactly the same way the words "living entity" and "Ego" are but a mode of expression for the presence of the five attachment groups, but when we come to examine the elements of being one by one, we discover that in the absolute sense there is no living entity there to form a basis for such figments as "I am," or "I"; . . .[9]

There being no security in things or self where all is changing, in flux, man in becoming, is uneasy, anxious, vulnerable, frustrated, suffering. This is the truth of Dukkha — man's on-going experience of life as unsatisfactory.

Having diagnosed the disease, the physician seeks to isolate its cause; he asks why existence in flux is unsatisfactory to man. In a word, the Buddha identified the cause of the arising of Dukkha (the Second Noble Truth) as desire (*tanha*), craving, thirst:

> This is the noble truth of the Origin of dukkha: It is this Craving (tanha) that leads to ever-fresh and repeated rebirth, and is connected with delight and pleasure, finding now here, now there its objects of enjoyment, namely: 1) Craving for sense pleasures, 2) Craving for continued becoming (existence), 3) Craving for self-annihilation after death.[10]

It is desire which gives rise to man's sense of self, 'I-ness', the desir*er*. 'I-ness' is self-perpetuating and escalating. The 'I' seeks to embellish its status, to satisfy its desires. Desire leads to attachment, a clinging to that which is desired, anxiety to attain and obtain — and aversion for that which is not desired. Attachment leads to disappointment and suffering in loss, in not achieving, in getting what one does not want. On analogy:

> The thirst of a thoughtless man grows like a creeper; he runs from life to life, like a monkey seeking fruit in the forest.[11]

Man 'becoming' is a seething mass of desire — greed (*raga*), hate (*dosa*), and delusion (*moha*) — a blazing, raging fire:

> Everything, brethren, is on fire. How, brethren, is everything on fire? The eye, brethren, is on fire, visible objects are on fire, the faculty of the eye is on fire, the sense of the eye is on fire, and also the sensation, whether pleasant or unpleasant or both, which arises from the sense of sight, is on fire. With what is it on fire? With the fire of passion (raga), of hate (dosa), of illu-

sion (moha), is it on fire, with birth, old age, death, grief, lamentation, suffering, sorrow and despair. Thus I declare. The ear is on fire, sounds are on fire. . . . The nose is on fire, scents are on fire. . . . The faculty of the mind is on fire. . . .[12]

Again, the Buddha spoke of the body with its sense organs as an open sore, a wound plagued with the discharge (*asava*) of sensuous desire, desire for existence, wrong views, and ignorance.[13]

The Buddha analyzed man's ceaseless striving in terms of a twelvefold chain of causation; desire is only a link in a cycle of dependent origination, a wheel of 'becoming': in ignorance — false sense of self, failure to comprehend and take seriously ceaseless change — man wills to act on his own behalf; willing to act gives rise to consciousness, the awareness of being (existing) which in turn gives rise to name and form, mind and body; mind and body extend sensory instruments occasioning contact with objects of sense — contact gives rise to sensation, sensation to desire; out of desire arises clinging, attachment, and as a result of clinging to self, objects of sense, other selves, man continues to become — the blazing fire is self-perpetuating as it devours the forest of sensory objects; 'becoming' cannot end in death for death itself is a moment of 'becoming', a moment full of desire and clinging, merely the moment of the beginning of the final decay of one gross form as the subtle energies blaze on to manifest a new form, a birth. And beings born, grow old and die; this is endless 'becoming', one link originating in dependence upon another and in turn inevitably giving rise to the next. We may also interpret the wheel of causation as representing 'becoming' in time: the ignorance and resulting volitions to act (accumulated action-energies) of the past occasion the consciousness, mind-body, sense organs, contact, sensations, desires, clinging, and 'becoming' of the present, and these in turn occasion the birth and growing old and dying of the future. Self-assertion is self-perpetuating

The Wheel of Becoming
(*bhava-cakka*)
Illustrating the Formula of Dependent Origination
(*paticca-samuppada*)

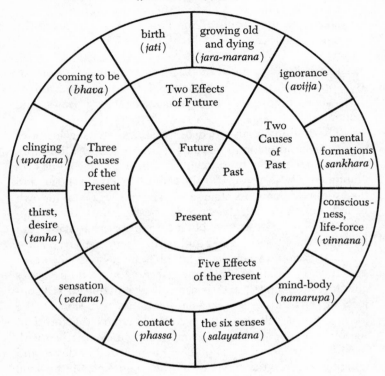

Sources: Dialogues of the Buddha. Sacred Books of the Buddhist Series. Maha Nidana Suttanta, T. W. Rhys Davids and C. A. F. Rhys Davids, trans., vol. 3, pp. 50–70; *Collection of the Middle-Length Sayings,* Sammaditthi Sutta, Lord Chalmers, trans., vol. 1, pp. 3–40; *Book of the Kindred Sayings,* Translation Series, Nidana-vagga, T. W. Rhys Davids, trans., vol. 2, pp. 1–94 passim.

and escalating — action begets reaction in human behavior as well as in the physical universe. Existence is endless grasping for self-aggrandizement, fulfillment, security, lasting happiness, perfection, but there is no finality in any of man's strivings. As long as he clings in hope of satisfying self through sensuous enjoyment and ideas he continues to be anxious and frustrated; he continues to suffer disappointment, 'pain, grief, and lamentation'.

Where there is no desire, there is no suffering. This is the Third Noble Truth, the truth of the cessation (*nirodha*) of desire, the truth of Nibbana (Sanskirt: *nirvana*):

> This is the Noble Truth of the Extinction of Dukkha: it is the complete fading away and extinction of this craving, its forsaking, giving up, the liberation and detachment from it.[14]

The goal, the 'salvation' of the way of the Buddha, is spoken of in the negative terms Nirodha ("cessation") and Nibbana ("blowing out, extinction"); the cessation of unsatisfactoriness, cessation of desiring; the blowing out of the blazing fire, extinction of the flame of self-assertion, extinction of greed, hatred, and delusion. When the Buddha was asked, "Where does the enlightened one, the realized, the one free from ignorance, free from desire, go after death?"; he answered, "Where does a fire go when deprived of fuel? It goes out." Nibbana is neither a place of eternal happiness after death (as heaven) nor is it simply annihilation. Words of positive definition fail — Nibbana is happiness, yet not the happiness conceived and sought by man in Dukkha, man desiring; it is the 'really real' yet not that reality which appears to one burdened with self. Nibbana is a quality of life. Nibbana is to be realized within, through following a path; it is not an idea or a place to be. Walpola Rahula, a Theravada monk, interprets Nibbana in a manner acceptable to most contemporary Buddhists:

> . . . Nirvana can be realized in this very life; it is not necessary to wait till you die to "attain" it.

He who has realized the Truth, Nirvana, is the happiest being in the world. He is free from all "complexes" and obsessions, the worries and troubles that torment others. His mental health is perfect. He does not repent the past, nor does he brood over the future. He lives fully in the present. Therefore he appreciates and enjoys things in the purest sense without self-projections. He is joyful, exultant, enjoying the pure life, his faculties pleased, free from anxiety, serene and peaceful. As he is free from selfish desire, hatred, ignorance, conceit, pride, and all such "defilements," he is pure and gentle, full of universal love, compassion, kindness, sympathy, understanding and tolerance. His service to others is of the purest, for he has no thought of self. He gains nothing, accumulates nothing, not even anything spiritual, because he is free from the illusion of Self, and the "thirst" for becoming.[15]

Knowing the disease, together with its cause and its contrasting nondisease (Nibbana), it remains to prescribe the way to recovery, the Fourth Noble Truth of the path to the cessation of Dukkha:

There are two extremes, monks, which he who has given up the world ought to avoid. What are these two extremes? A life given to pleasures, devoted to pleasures and lusts — this is degrading, sensual, vulgar, ignoble, and profitless.

And a life given to mortifications — this is painful, ignoble, and profitless.

By avoiding these two extremes, monks, the Tathagata has gained the knowledge of the Middle Path which leads to insight, which leads to wisdom, which conduces to calm, to knowledge, to Sambodhi (Supreme Enlightenment), to Nibbana.

Which, monks, is this Middle Path the knowledge of which the Tathagata has gained, which leads to insight, which leads to wisdom, which conduces to calm, to knowledge, to Sambodhi, to Nibbana?

It is the Noble Eightfold Path, namely: right views, right intent, right speech, right conduct, right means of livelihood, right endeavor, right mindfulness, right meditation.

This, monks, is the Middle Path the knowledge of which the Tathagata has gained, which leads to insight, which leads to wisdom, which conduces to calm, to knowledge, to perfect enlightenment, to Nibbana.[16]

This Middle Path between hedonism and asceticism[17] is a way of self-discipline toward the cessation of desire and the acquisition of insight (*vipassana*); it is a way of going, in thought, feeling, word, and deed, conducive to the reduction of wrong action (*akusala-kamma*) and the production of right action (*kusala-kamma*), and eventuating in the cessation of all action-energies which occasion continued rebirth and redeath.

The eight factors of the path are generalized as threefold: right speech, action, and livelihood being matters of ethical conduct (*sila*); right effort, mindfulness, and concentration being matters of mental development (*samadhi*); and right views and intent being matters of wisdom (*panna*).[18] Sila and Samadhi are means; Paññā is both means and end. The three are to develop simultaneously — thus the eight factors are not successive stages to be perfected one after another or rungs on a ladder to be climbed; rather, they go hand in hand as aspects of an all-encompassing conditioning process.

The critical element of the path is mindfulness (*sati*):

The one and only path, Bhikkhus ["Buddhist monks"], leading to the purification of beings, to passing far beyond grief and lamentation, to the dying-out of ill and misery, to the attainment of right method, to the realization of Nirvana [Nibbana], is that of the Fourfold Setting up of Mindfulness.[19]

The mind is the key instrument toward the control of desire and the arising of insight — Dukkha, its cause and its cure must be penetrated, fully realized; greed, hatred, and delusion must be seen for what they are. The final goal of mental development is not the total exclusion or transcendence of the awareness of the three factors of existence (impermanence, unsatisfactoriness, and soullessness) in deep trance, but perfect insight into these factors.

Mindfulness has two aspects: simple awareness (bare attention) and comprehension, the former leading into the latter. Simple awareness is dispassionate attentiveness to, the objectification of, what one is, does, says, and thinks.

> By Bare Attention we understand the clear and single-minded awareness of what actually happens *to* us and *in* us, at the successive moments of perception. It is called "bare" because it attends to the bare facts of a perception without reacting to them by deed, speech, or mental comment.[20]

The classic statement on mindfulness is the Mahasatipatthana Suttanta, and here mindfulness is directed fourfold: to body, feelings, thoughts, and ideas:

> Herein, O bhikkhus, a brother, as to the body, continues so to look upon the body, that he remains ardent, self-possessed and mindful, having overcome both the hankering and the dejection common in the world. And in the same way as to feelings, thoughts and ideas, he so looks upon each, that he remains ardent, self-possessed and mindful, having overcome the hankering and the dejection that is common in the world. This is what is called right mindfulness.[21]

Mindfulness of body entails attention to breathing — awareness of the 'experience' of breathing in and out, and the cultivation of measured breathing. It entails giving attention to the composition of the body — its hair, color, bones, sinew, and the like — and to the decomposition of the body, the body in the process of decaying after death:

He keeps on considering how the body is something that comes to be, or again he keeps on considering how the body is something that passes away; or again he keeps on considering the coming to be with the passing away. . . .[22]

Mindfulness of body entails attention to the activities of the body — walking, sitting, standing, lying down, eating, drinking, talking, and so forth:

. . . whether he departs or returns, whether he looks at or looks away from, whether he has drawn in or stretched out (his limbs), whether he has donned under-robe, over-robe, or bowl, whether he is eating, drinking, chewing, reposing, or whether he is obeying the calls of nature — (he) is aware of what he is about. . . . In going, standing, sitting, sleeping, watching, talking, or keeping silence, he knows what he is doing.[23]

Continuous, bare attention 'objectifies' the body, its internal processes and external activities. Through mindfulness one becomes intensely but impersonally aware and ceases to understand the body and its actions as 'me' and 'mine' — he comprehends impermanence, Dukkha, and soullessness with respect to body.

Just so, one must develop mindfulness of feelings — feelings of pleasure and feelings of pain; mindfulness of thoughts — thoughts of lust, thoughts of hate; and mindfulness of ideas (*dhamma*) — meaning concepts and teachings. In the latter, one takes as his object such matters as the Buddha's teaching concerning the five aggregates of human existence (matter, sensations, perception, mental formations, and consciousnesses), the Four Noble Truths or the four sublime states: loving-kindness or friendship (*metta*), sympathetic joy, joy for other's welfare (*mudita*), compassion (*karuna*), and equanimity (*upekkha*). Mindfulness of the sublime states brings into focus the 'positive' dimension of the Buddha's path, the inevitable result of the giving up of greed, hatred, and delusion.

Mindfulness is supported by and conducive to the other elements of the Eightfold Path. As to Sila: right speech is speaking the truth, and refraining from gossip and unkind, vain, and frivolous talk; right action is refraining from taking life, stealing, and sexual misconduct; and right means of livelihood is refraining from violent occupations such as trading in weapons, intoxicating beverages, and flesh (slave trade, prostitution, and raising animals for slaughter). As to mental development, mindfulness is supported by and conducive to right effort and right concentration:

> There are these Four Great Efforts: The effort to a) restrain unprofitable states of mind (that would otherwise lead to evil acts), b) to abandon the unprofitable states of mind, c) to develop, and d) to maintain the risen profitable states of mind and make them grow.[24]

Right concentration is the quieting of the mind through the cultivation of one-pointedness, this being achieved by focusing the mind on a single point (a sense-object such as the flame of a candle or a hole in the wall or a mental image). Through concentration one may pass into one or more of the Absorptions or Raptures (*jhana*):

> Then estranged from lusts, aloof from evil dispositions, he enters into and remains in the First Rapture — a state of *joy and ease* born of detachment, *reasoning and investigation going on* the while. . . .
>
> Then further . . . suppressing all reasoning and investigation (he) enters into and abides in the Second Jhana, a state of *joy and ease*, born of the serenity of concentration, when *no reasoning or investigation goes on*, — a state of elevation of mind, a tranquillisation of the heart within. . . .
>
> Then further . . . holding *aloof from joy*, (he) becomes equable; and mindful and self-possessed he experiences in his body that *ease* which the Arahats talk of when they say: "The man serene and self-possessed is well at

ease," and so he enters into and abides in the Third Jhana. . . .

Then further . . . by *putting away alike of ease and of pain,* by the passing away alike of any elation, any dejection, he had previously felt, (he) enters into and abides in the Fourth Jhana, a state of *pure self-possession and equanimity, without pain and without ease.*[25]

Beyond these four absorptions, termed absorptions with form (*rupa-jhana*), he may pass to the level of formless absorptions (*arupa-jhana*), the realization successively of the infinity of space, the infinity of consciousness, nothingness, and finally the state of neither perception nor nonperception.[26] Beyond the four form-absorptions one may also pass into possession of one or more special psychic powers (*iddhi*) such as the ability to change form and place at will, pass through solid objects, recall former births.[27] Whatever the achievement as to levels of absorption and psychic powers, the intended end of concentration is tranquillity of mind as one proceeds toward insight.[28] Passing through the absorptions is accessory to but not essential to the wisdom which is full or perfect comprehension of impermanence, unsatisfactoriness, and soullessness — the complete cessation of ignorance and desire.

This brings us to the wisdom (*panna*) aspects of the Eightfold Path: right views (understanding) and right intent (resolve). Right understanding refers both to the preliminary comprehension of the Four Noble Truths with which comprehension one undertakes the path and to the penetrating insight into the true nature of existence which proceeds from right conduct and mental development. Likewise, right resolve is both the initial resolve to undertake and persevere on the path and the perfected will, free from lust, ill will, and violence and firmly resolved to renunciation, goodwill, and compassion.

Short of perfect insight in this life and thus the cessation of 'becoming' beyond death, the wise man looks to the conditioning of a favorable rebirth; or, to state it another

way, he seeks to enhance his 'merit-status'. We have spoken
of man's 'becoming' in rebirth and redeath as conditioned by
Kamma (action). There are three kinds of Kamma: right
(*kusala*) or meritorious (*punna*); wrong (*akusala*) or de-
meritorious (*papa*); and neutral, nonfruit-producing
(*aphala*).

> His good deeds and his wickedness,
> Whate'er a mortal does while here;
> T'is this that he can call his own,
> This with him take as he goes hence.
> This is what follows after him,
> And like a shadow ne'er departs.

> Let all, then, noble deeds perform,
> A treasure-store for future weal;
> For merit gained this life within,
> Will yield a blessing in the next.[29]

The Eightfold Path is a means of "burning up" accumulated
demerit, avoiding further demerit, and of accumulating
merit. Rebirth may be again at the human level or at one of
thirty other levels of being in a multileveled universe.

Scripture and tradition correlate levels of spiritual
awareness or psychic states and levels of existence. These
levels may be perceived "subjectively" as dimensions of insight or "objectively" as places of residence (heavens, hells,
etc.), each inhabited by distinctive beings. The Buddha's
psychoanalytic concern with self-awareness is not contra-
dicted by popular mythology because it is understood that
the same reality may be perceived variously according to
individual insight-level. The sophisticated meditator understands that gods, demons, and ghosts are personifications of
desires, anxieties, fears, and ignorance and does not depre-
cate the man of less sophistication who objectifies and personifies, who gives gross form to the same realities. The Pali
scriptures keep these perceptions together throughout. Thus,
Gotama's struggle with himself preceding enlightenment is
objectified as Gotama versus Mara, the Evil One. While the

Buddha, both pre- and post-enlightenment, is clearly self-sufficient, in command of all, he is constantly served by gods, spirits, and animals, e.g., by the spirit of the gate at the renunciation; by Sakka, Chief of the gods (*deva*) of the second heaven, as valet just following the enlightenment; and by Mucalinda, King of snakes, sheltering the Buddha during a rainstorm. He is counseled by Brahma Sahampati, Lord of the Brahmā-lokas ("Realms of Brahma"), as he ponders whether or not to go forth and preach following enlightenment.[30] There is no doubt that the gods, demons, and ghosts are subordinate to the Enlightened One. The Buddha is teacher of both "gods and men" and, on occasion, teacher of animals.[31] He visits the heavens, on one occasion preaching to his mother in the heaven of the thirty-three Devas.[32] The gods are constantly on hand to hear the Buddha's preaching to his human-form disciples. Brahma and Sakka, chiefs over the gods, praise and honor the Buddha with the words:

> The Three-and-Thirty, verily, both gods and lord, rejoice,
> Tathagata they honour and the cosmic law sublime.[33]

Human existence is one of mixed pleasure and pain. Below man, in descending order and increasing pain of punishment, are the demons, the hungry ghosts (spirits of the dead undergoing punishment), the animals, and the inhabitants of the hells. Above man, in order of increasing pleasure, are the twenty-two levels of gods, the first six levels of which together with man comprise the Realm of Sensuous Bliss. The beings of the Realm of Sensuous Bliss together with the beings of the four levels of punishment make up the Realm of Sensuous Pleasure (*kama-loka*). The remaining sixteen levels of the gods make up the Realm of Form (*rupa-loka*). Beyond is the Realm of the Formless (*arupa-loka*), the four levels of the formless absorptions.[34] The Form and Formless Realms are known as the Realms of Brahma (*Brahma-loka*).

Human existence in mixed pleasure and pain permits the greatest possibility for the attainment of Nibbana. The gods are too engrossed in pleasure to attend to the discipline of the Eightfold Path or merit-making, and the inhabitants of the levels of punishment are undergoing too much pain. Beings reside in the various realms according to merit and demerit, good and bad Kamma. Men who live dominated by anger, hate, and violence will be punished in the hells. Those dominated by concern for food and sex will undergo punishment in animal forms, and those dominated by greed will suffer as hungry ghosts in the purgatories.[35] The doers of good works will enjoy rebirth in a more favorable human form or as gods in one of the heavens of the Kama-loka. Those who meditate and attain the absorptions will be reborn in one of the Brahma-lokas appropriate to their attainment. According to another classification, those who undertake the path of the Buddha may attain the level of: a Stream-enterer (*sotapanna*) and upon death never be reborn below the human state; a Once-returner (*sakadagamin*) and upon death return to the human state never to be born again; or a Nonreturner (*anagamin*), reborn in a Brahma-loka from whence he attains Nibbana.[36] It must be kept in mind that rebirth in any of the realms is only a relative pleasure or pain — it is to remain within the universe of 'becoming' and short of the bliss of Nibbana. The Buddha, reflecting on a former life, noted:

> I taught my disciples the way to communion with the Brahma-world. But, . . . that religious life did not conduce to detachment, to passionlessness, to cessation of craving, to peace, to understanding, to insight of the higher stages of the Path, to Nirvana, but only to rebirth in the Brahma-world.[37]

As is evident with the Buddha and the gods, the beings of the various levels of existence can be aware of and affected by each other's movements and to those humans unprotected by the power of insight (great merit) the movements of nonhuman beings, especially demons and hungry ghosts, may have adverse as well as auspicious effects. The Buddha and those who have achieved a high degree of self-

Nirvana
Unconditioned, Uncompounded

FORMLESS REALM	Neither Perception nor Nonperception	
	Nothingness	Obtained by entry on the formless concentrations.
	Infinite Consciousness	
	Infinite Space	
REALM OF FORM	The Heavens of Form (16-fold)	Obtained by entry on the form-concentrations.
	The Heavens of Sensuous Desire (6-fold)	Attained by the practice of the eight precepts and some meditation.
	Man ↗ (evolution) ↘ (degeneration)	Maintained by keeping the five precepts pure.
REALM OF DESIRE / 4-fold Realm of Punishment	Titans (asuras)	The result of grasping after power.
	Hungry Ghosts (peta)	The result of preoccupation with attachments to family, money, possessions.
	Animals	The result of having thought only for food and sex.
	Hell-sprites	The result of anger, hatred, and violence.

Superhuman Levels — the Gods → increasing happiness and equanimity →

Human pleasure-pain

Subhuman Levels ← increasing pain ←

The Realm of Conditioned and Compounded Events — The World of Birth and Death

Source: Adapted from B. Khantipalo, *What Is Buddhism?*

mastery are capable of 'perceiving' ('psyching-out') non-human beings[38] and cannot be ill-affected by their movements. On one occasion, Sariputta, one of the most venerated of the Buddha's disciples, sat in meditation —

> And it chanced that two demons, who were comrades, were passing on some errand from the northern quarter of the heavens to the southern. And these demons saw the venerable Sariputta, on the moonlight night, seated under the open sky, with freshly shaven head. And at the sight of him, the first demon spoke to the second demon as follows:
>
> "It occurs to me, comrade, that it would be a fine plan to give this monk a blow on the head." . . . [he] gave the venerable Sariputta a blow on the head. With such a blow one might fell an elephant seven or seven-and-a-half cubits high, or might split a mountain peak. Thereupon, with the cry, "I am burning! I am burning!" the demon fell from where he stood into hell. And the venerable Moggallana the Great . . . saw the demon . . . and having drawn near, he spoke to the venerable Sariputta as follows:
>
> "Are you comfortable, brother? Are you doing well? Does nothing trouble you?"
>
> "I am comfortable, brother Moggallana. I am doing well . . . but my head troubles me a little."[39]

Sariputta's power over the demon was passive. On a number of occasions the Buddha actively exercised power over spirits chanting verses of protection (*paritta*) which he then encouraged his followers to use whenever appropriate. The Buddha employed the Ratana Paritta, for instance, to conquer and disperse malevolent spirits who had brought famine and plague to the city of Vesali. The Paritta makes appeal to the power of the three jewels (*ti-ratana*) — Buddha, Dhamma, and Sangha:

> Whatever beings are assembled here
> — So be they native to the earth or sky — ,

Come, let us laud the Enlightened One, thus-gone,
Honoured of gods and men: May there be safety.

Whatever beings are assembled here
— So be they native to the earth or sky — ,
Come, let us laud the True Ideal, thus-gone,
Honoured of gods and men: May there be safety.

Whatever beings are assembled here
— So be they native to the earth or sky — ,
Come, let us laud the Community, thus-gone,
Honoured of gods and men: May there be safety.[40]

The Buddha delivered the Atanatiya Paritta on being asked
to issue a word of protection against Yakkhas (fairies, sprites,
demons) who, because they did not believe in the Buddha,
might attack his followers. The lengthy Paritta is followed
by the Buddha's exhortation:

There are creatures not human, . . . who are rough, iras-
cible, violent. They heed neither the . . . kings, nor the
officers of the kings, nor their men. . . . This . . . is the
ward rune, whereby both brethren and sisters of the
Order, and laymen and laywomen may dwell at ease,
guarded, protected, and unscathed. When any brother
or sister, layman or laywoman, shall have well learnt this
Atanata [a town] spell, and shall know it word-per-
fectly, if any non-human creature, whether it be a Yakkha of either sex, young or otherwise, chief or attendant,
or servant, or a Gandhabba [heavenly musician], or a
Kumbhanda [celestial being], or a Naga, of either sex,
young or otherwise, chief or attendant or servant, should
approach him or her while walking, standing, sitting or
lying down, with malevolent intent, such a creature, . . .
would not win, either in village or township, hospitality
or respect.[41]

When the Buddha is told of the death of a monk due to
snakebite he issues another Paritta saying:

Monks, I allow you to suffuse with loving-kindness of mind these four royal snake families, (and) to make a charm (paritta) for the self for self-protection, for self-guarding.

[the charm:]

Love from me for the footless,
Love for the two-footed from me,
Love from me for the four-footed,
Love for the many-footed from me.

Do not let the footless harm me,
Do not let the two-footed harm me,
Do not let the four-footed harm me,
Do not let the many-footed harm me.

May all beings, all breathers, all creatures
      every one,
See all lucky things; may no evil whatever come.

Immeasurable is the Awakened One, immeasurable
      Dhamma, immeasurable the Order.
Limited are creeping things; snakes, scorpions,
      centipedes, spinning spiders, lizards, mice.

A protection has been made by me, a charm
      made by me;
Let the creatures withdraw.
I, even I, honour the Lord,
I honour the seven fully self-awakened Ones.[42]

The Mahamangala Paritta which in effect is a recitation of the Buddha's prescriptions for the lay life, is the most powerful protective word of all:

> Since by working suchlike (omens)
> Men are everywhere unvanquished
> And go everywhere in safety,
> That is their supreme good omen.[43]

The Parittas are intended to ward off any harm which might come intentionally or unintentionally from nonhuman beings disposed toward trouble-making and malevolent acts. The gods (*deva*) are considered to be well disposed toward followers of the Buddha and especially so if they receive somewhat regular offerings from men. On more than one occasion the Buddha exhorted his followers to make such offerings:

> Wheresoe'er the prudent man shall take up his abode, let him support there good and upright men of self-control.
>
> Let him make offerings to all such deities as may be there. Revered, they will revere him; honoured, they honour him again;
>
> Are gracious to him as a mother to the son of her womb. And a man who has the grace of the gods, good fortune he beholds.[44]

Offerings to the Devas are one of the five offerings (*dakkhina*) or gifts (*dana*) to be made regularly by laymen.[45] Offerings are also to be made to another type of nonhuman being, the Hungry Ghost (*peta*) who may be a dead kinsmen. In this case, however, the offering is to be made not because the ghosts are well (or ill) disposed, but because they are badly in need of merit and can only receive it when it is offered or transferred to them by men and through the monk. The Tirokudda-Sutta of the Khuddaka-patha ("Little Readings") of the Pali Canon is entirely given over to the Buddha's exhortation to transfer merit (*anumodana*) to the Petas. Another section of the Pali Canon is composed entirely of stories of the Petas (Peta-vatthu — "Tales of Hungry Ghosts"). In the first story it is said:

> The holy saints are to be compared to the extensive field of merit, the givers to the cultivators, the gifts and offerings to the seeds, and the efficacy to the harvest resulting from the down-pourings of rain-water. The seeds

nurtured by rain-water in the cultivated field of merit bear fruits to both the dead kinsmen and the giver, the departed spirits enjoy the fruits, and the giver too prospers with merit. Performing a meritorious deed here in relation to the living kinsmen and the religious institutions and honouring the dead as well, the pious giver proceeds to heaven after having done a good deed on the earth.[46]

As is the case with most lay acts of giving or offerings, the offerings are made through the monks rather than directly to the dead. Gifts to the monks are most merit-full since the merit-power of the offering depends upon the purity of the receiver as well as that of the giver. The Peta-vatthu also recommends, however, gifts to the unfortunate and 'acts of public utility' such as providing drinking water for the thirsty, digging wells and constructing reservoirs, and building bridges.[47] The exhortations of the Buddha to make offerings for the dead are as much or more concerned with encouraging acts of giving for the welfare of the Sangha and society and the future of the giver as with the release of the ghosts from purgatory. The stories of the Peta-vatthu vividly portray the anguish of the dead in the purgatories as a warning to the living lest their fate be likewise.

> . . . the gift which is made to the Holy Order is well established in it, and turns out to be of benefit to them (the petas) for a long time to come, and reaches them. By this act, a social service is done to the living kinsmen, a great honour is given to the bhikkhus, and as for yourselves, no mean joy of merit you gain.[48]

III

The Sangha

THE BUDDHA encouraged followers of two general types: those who, like himself, renounced the 'worldly' life of settled society and those who remained in the householder's estate. The former, among the many recluses of northeast India, came to be distinctively known as *bhikkhu*[1] (fem.: *bhikkhuni*) — "one who has received the higher ordination" — or *samanera* (fem.: *samaneri*) — "one who has received the novitiate ordination." The latter are designated as *upasaka* (fem.: *upasika*) — "layman," or *gahapati,* "householder." While the Eightfold Path reflects the Buddha's own experience in renunciation of the worldly life and was initially addressed to the recluse, the path is understood to generalize the way open to both monk and lay followers — the former engaging more intensely than the latter. The Buddha conceived of the pursuit of Nibbana by layman and monk as fully complimentary and reciprocal — the layman pursuing the goal in such a way as to provide the material necessities of life to the monk and the monk giving of himself to the layman by way of maintaining and manifesting the inspiring ideal and teaching and guiding the layman. To the layman, and Bhikkhu is the zenith:

In five ways should the clansman minister to recluses and brahmins as the zenith: — by affection in act and speech and mind; by keeping open house to them, by supplying their temporal needs.

Thus ministered to as the zenith, recluses and brahmins show their love for the clansman in six ways: — they restrain him from evil, they exhort him to good, they love him with kindly thoughts, they teach him what he has not heard, they correct and purify what he has heard, they reveal to him the way to heaven.[2]

The Bhikkhu is a 'reservoir of merit' for the lay society, providing the layman with the good word, inspiration of character and wisdom, and the opportunity for giving good gifts. He goes forth:

> . . . for the gain of the many, for the welfare of the many, out of compassion for the world, for the good, for the gain, and for the welfare of gods and men.[3]

The layman may not attain perfect insight in this life but through the Bhikkhu he may ensure a better rebirth, i.e., one of enjoyment in a heaven or one as a man prepared to undertake the Bhikkhu-way.

The Bhikkhu-way

Sangha, literally "gathering," may refer to the entire following of the Buddha, both lay and monastic; but it is most frequently employed with reference only to the gathered body of Bhikkhus. The way of the Bhikkhu is not one of severe asceticism, but it does require rigorous self-discipline, apart from the cares, attachments, and temptations of the householder's life:

> . . . forsaking his portion of wealth, be it great or small, forsaking his circle of relatives, be they many or be they few, he cuts off his hair and beard, he clothes himself

in the orange-colored robes, and he goes forth from the household life into the homeless state.[4]

The Buddha is said to have instituted the Bhikkhu-Sangha when, following his first sermon at the deer park near Benares, five fellow wanderers decided to take up his path. The earliest texts on the act of ordination to the Sangha emphasize only the candidate's taking of the threefold refuge:

> Let him (who desires to receive the ordination), first have his hair and beard cut off; let him put on yellow robes, adjust his upper robe so as to cover one shoulder, salute the feet of the Bhikkhus (with his head), and sit down squatting; then let him raise his joined hands and tell him to say:
> "I take my refuge in the Buddha, I take my refuge in the Dhamma, I take my refuge in the Sangha" [repeated three times].[5]

As time passed, experience dictated a more demanding standard for Sangha admission. One who would undertake the Bhikkhu-life must make formal request to a duly constituted body of Bhikkhus. The Buddha prescribed two levels of ordination, the *pabbajja* or novice (*samanera*) ordination, and the *upasampada* or higher (*bhikkhu*) ordination. According to the Vinaya text, no one under the age of fifteen years[6] may receive the *pabbajja* and no one under twenty, the higher ordination.[7] Further, to be ordained, one must be a human being,[8] have the permission of his parents or wife, be free of debt, and free of disease; he must be a freeman, not in the employ of government, and must have his own alms-bowl and robes.[9] The beginning novice or Bhikkhu must have a preceptor (*upajjhaya*) and a teacher (*acariya*) — Bhikkhus who have completed at least ten years since their higher ordination — who consent to guide his progress in the monastic life and whom he serves in everyday personal matters. While the preceptor is primarily responsible for the ordination itself and the personal conduct of the new monk and the teacher for his education, their relationship to the newly ordained is defined in the same way:

> The upajjhaya, O Bhikkhus, ought to consider the sad-dhiviharika (i.e. pupil) as a son; the saddhiviharika ought to consider the upajjhaya as a father. Thus these two, united by mutual reverence, confidence, and communion of life, will progress, advance, and reach a high stage in this doctrine and discipline (dhamma-vinaya).[10]

An act of ordination is valid only if at least ten Bhikkhus are present and the ordaining Bhikkhu has completed at least ten years from his higher ordination.

In ordination, the novice undertakes to keep ten basic precepts:

He vows:

1. Not to destroy life
2. Not to steal
3. Not to engage in sexual misconduct
4. Not to lie
5. Not to take alcoholic beverages
6. Not to eat at forbidden times
7. Not to participate in dancing, singing, music, and the observance of shows
8. Not to wear garlands, perfumes, unguents, ornaments, and finery
9. Not to use high or wide beds
10. Not to accept gold or silver (money)

The Bhikkhu must commit himself to keep all two hundred and twenty-seven rules and regulations prescribed in the Patimokkha in the Vinaya text of the Pali Canon. The prescription concerns what is prohibited and is divided eightfold into:

1. Four cases involving defeat (exclusion from the order):

    a) Sexual intercourse with human or animal
    b) Taking that which is not given (stealing)
    c) Taking the life of a human being, hiring an assassin, or desiring the death of another person
    d) Falsely claiming to have attained certain insight and/or power through meditation

2. Thirteen cases requiring meetings of the community of monks in both the early and later stages of the case,[11] and covering such matters as:
    a) Various relationships with the opposite sex short of sexual intercourse
    b) Malice toward another monk
    c) Having a residence erected in an improper place and without the approval of the Sangha
    d) Causing dissension and division in the order
    e) Refusing to accept comment or criticism from fellow Bhikkhus

3. Two cases, involving contact with a woman, in which cases the infraction must be clarified

4. Thirty cases requiring expiation (repentance) and forfeiture of goods, medicines, or money wrongly accepted

5. Ninety-two cases of offenses requiring expiation, e.g., using abusive language or occasioning ill will by speaking disrespectfully of another Bhikkhu

6. Four cases concerning the taking of food in which the infraction ought to be confessed

7. Seventy-five rules of conduct, infraction of which is considered improper, e.g., being properly clad when making the alms-round for food

8. Seven rules regarding the settlement of cases

    When he has thus become a recluse he passes a life self-restrained by that restraint which should be binding on a recluse. Uprightness is his delight, and he sees danger in the least of those things he should avoid. He adopts and trains himself in the precepts. He encompasses himself with goodness in word and deed. He sustains his life by means that are quite pure; good is his conduct, guarded the door of his senses; mindful and self-possessed, he is altogether happy![12]

The Vinaya prescribes that the Bhikkhus of each chapter of monks (all those of higher ordination residing within a given boundary — *sima*) recite the Patimokkha rules twice each lunar month on the new-moon and full-moon Uposatha ("preparatory observance")[13] days.[14] The recitation is occasion for each monk to declare himself pure or guilty of an offense. Minor infractions of the rules are simply dismissed with their recognition by the offender. In the case of major infractions, the entire monk community may come together to take disciplinary proceedings against the offender who may be rebuked, temporarily subordinated to an overseer, or excommunicated, made to ask pardon, or placed on probation.[15]

Acts requiring the gathering of the Sangha community are valid only when the complete chapter of Bhikkhus is gathered — those ill or otherwise indisposed must send word through another Bhikkhu. Further, a certain minimum number of Bhikkhus must be present for the valid transaction of business or performance of rituals — twenty or more Bhikkhus may perform all Sangha acts (Sanghakamma); fewer than twenty but at least ten may perform all acts but an *abbhana,* the rehabilitation of a monk who has been excommunicated; five to nine Bhikkhus may perform all acts except the higher ordination and Abbhana; and four Bhikkhus may perform all acts but the *pavarana* ("confessions of offenses"), higher ordination, and Abbhana.[16]

At the beginning of the rainy season (Vassa), either the day after the full moon of *asalha* (June–July) or one month after that full moon, all Bhikkhus and Bhikkhunis[17] must enter into retreat for three months. They are to cease their wanderings and take up residence in their home monastery, going out only under unusual circumstances (e.g., serious illness of a relative) from which they must return within seven days. The end of the rainy season retreat is marked by a special meeting of the Sangha to share confession of offenses. This is known as Pavarana.[18]

Then follows Kathina, the acquisition of new robes. The Vinaya text allows that robes may be made up by the monks themselves or offered to them by the laity. The latter is encouraged:

> Now we [laymen] will bestow gifts (on the Bhikkhus) and acquire merit by good works, since the Blessed One has allowed the Bhikkhus to wear lay robes.[19]

The monk is permitted to have three robes — a single undergarment, a double waist cloth, and a single upper robe. In addition, he may have a rain-bathing cloth, a water-straining cloth, and a bag in which to carry his alms-bowl.[20]

The material needs of the monk are few. In addition to clothing, he requires only food, medicine, and housing, all of which should be supplied to him by the laity. The Bhikkhu should look upon these four requisites as purely instrumental to a larger end, as medicine for a wound (the body):

> . . . they who have retired from the world are not fond of their bodies; but, without being attached to them, they take care of their bodies in order to advance in the religious life. The body . . . has been likened to a wound by The Blessed One; and, therefore, they who have retired from the world take care of their bodies as though they were wounds, without thereby becoming attached to them.[21]

He is to make no long-range provision for these necessities, but receive them from day to day as they come. Nor does he delight in them or feel sad when he is without them:

> Wherefore, brethren, thus should ye train yourselves: —
> "We will be contented with no matter what robes, alms,

lodging, medical equipment. We will commend contentment with such, nor because of any one of them will we commit anything that is unseemly or unfit. If we have not gotten a robe, alms or the rest, we will not be perturbed; if we have gotten, we will enjoy it without clinging or infatuation, committing no fault, discerning danger, wise as to escape."[22]

Except as he is invited to take food in the homes of the laity, the Bhikkhu is to receive it while wandering through the village. This food-gathering (*pindapata*) act is to be at one and the same time an exercise in self-discipline of mind and body and a provision of opportunity for the laity to make merit:

> . . . take pattern by the moon when ye go a-begging, hold aloof both in body and in mind, never weary your welcome, nor be impudent to your benefactors.[23]

> Verily, brethren, if a brother go among the families with such a mind: — "Let them only give! Let them not refuse to give! Let them only give to me abundantly, not scantily! Let them give me excellent things only, not poor things! Let them only give quickly, not tardily! Let them only give to me respectfully, not disrespectfully!" — he, going among the families with such thoughts, if they give not, is vexed, and he feels pain and sorrow because of that. So does he feel if they give scantily, if they give poor things, if they give tardily, if they give disrespectfully. This manner of brother is unworthy to go among the families.[24]

> . . . that brother, whose heart when he goes among the families does not sink down, or get seized or bound, but thinks: Let them who desire gains gain! Let them who desire merit work merit! Let a man be pleased and joyous at the gains of others, even as he is pleased and joyous at his own gains! This manner of brother is worthy to go among the families.[25]

A wide variety of foodstuffs are permitted the Bhikkhu — the only major restrictions being against his partaking of alcoholic beverages and meat which has been specially prepared for him.[26] He may not eat the flesh of a human, an elephant, horse, dog, snake, lion, tiger, or hyena.[27] Food is to be partaken of in moderation and without delight in its taste or smell.

The Bhikkhu withdraws from family, friends, and the larger society to undertake a strict discipline; nonetheless and thereby he undertakes a responsibility for the world. Scripture, in effect, prescribes daily contact between the monk and the laity (through food-gathering) and constant interaction between Bhikkhu and laity as the Bhikkhu fulfills a commitment to preach and to teach. He is to:

> wander, for the gain of the many, for the welfare of the many, out of compassion for the world, for the good, for the gain, and for the welfare of gods and men. [He is to] Preach . . . the doctrine which is glorious in the beginning, glorious in the middle, glorious at the end, in the spirit and in the letter; proclaim a consummate, perfect, and pure life of holiness.[28]

The good he fosters is fostered passively. His power lies in his presence as a man of purity and wisdom. His very existence calls forth respect, reverence, and meritorious deeds:

> There are these *twenty personal qualities*, making up the Samanaship of a Samana [Bhikkhu], *and these two outward signs*, by reason of which the Samana is worthy of salutation, and of respect, and of reverence. And what are they? The best form of self-restraint, the highest kind of self-control, right conduct, calm manners, mastery over (his deeds and words), . . . etc. recitation (of the Scriptures), asking questions (of those wise in the Dhamma and Vinaya), rejoicing in the Silas. . .[29]

The two outward signs are ". . . the wearing of the yellow robe, and the being shaven."[30] The Bhikkhu is respected and reverenced by the laity whether or not he is accomplished in the discipline, i.e., possesses the twenty personal qualities; he is respected even by a layman who himself may be more accomplished in the discipline than the Bhikkhu:

> It is because he [the layman] sees him [the Bhikkhu] to be in the company of those in whom all evil has been destroyed, . . . because he knows that he has joined the noblest brotherhood, . . . because he knows that he listens to the recitation of the Patimokkha, . . . because he knows that he wears the outward signs of Samanaship, and carries out the intention of the Buddha . . . that the converted' [accomplished] layman thinks it right to do reverence, and to show respect to the unconverted [unaccomplished] Bhikkhu.[31]

The Bhikkhu is committed to preach and to teach the way of the Buddha. More than this he is to:

> . . . restrain him [the layman] from evil, . . . exhort him to good, . . . love him with kindly thoughts, . . . reveal to him the way to heaven.[32]

In particular, he is to follow the Buddha's example, if not his express command, to counsel the laity on worldly affairs, heal the sick, and command malevolent spirits.[33] In all of these matters the Bhikkhu is to proceed without 'ego-involvement', without selfish interest, and only when the layman seeks him out. He passively influences, preaches, teaches, counsels, and heals as the layman comes out to offer food, invites the Bhikkhu into his home, attends observances at the monastery and asks the Bhikkhu's advice.

The Way of the Laity

Whosoever, in this world gives gifts, and lives in righteousness, and keeps Uposatha, he, glad, right glad, joyful, cheerful, happy, becomes filled with a sweet sense

of trust and bliss ruling in his heart; his goodness grows
still more and more abundantly. Like a deep pool of
clear water, ... and into which on one side the spring
pours, while on the other the water flows away; so as it
flows away it comes again, and there can be no failure
there — so . . . does his goodness grow more and more
abundantly.[34]

> . . . he has practised so as to conquer both worlds;
> he tastes success both in this world and in the next.[35]

The layman, limited by the necessities of 'worldly' involvement, labors in terms of more modest goals than those of the
Bhikkhu. Scripture defines that which he is to seek in and
through this life as fourfold: wealth, honor, long life, and
rebirth in one of the heavens.[36] Wealth is to be actively pursued and enjoyed but in a manner conducive rather than
detrimental to honor, long life, and the attainment of heaven.
This means, in brief, that wealth is to be pursued and enjoyed in keeping with the five-precepts ethic and as essentially the basis of meritorious acts. The layman strives with a
view to the attainment of four perfections: perfection of
faith — ". . . faith in the enlightenment of the Tathagata (the
Buddha)"; perfection of virtue — the keeping of the five
precepts; perfection of generosity — he ". . . lives at home
with heart free from the taint of stinginess, he is open-
handed, delighting in self-surrender, one to ask a favour of,
one who delights in dispensing charitable gifts"; and the perfection of wisdom — ". . . knowing coveting and wrong desire to be a depravity of the mind, (he) casts out the mind's
depravities of malice . . . sloth-and-topor . . . distraction-and-
flurry . . . doubt-and-wavering."[37]

The five precepts are the foundation of the lay ethic:

> When a man with trusting heart takes upon himself the
> precepts — abstinence from destroying life; abstinence
> from taking what has not been given; abstinence from

evil conduct in respect of lusts; abstinence from lying words; abstinence from strong, intoxicating, maddening drinks, the root of carelessness — that is a sacrifice better than open largesse, better than perpetual alms, better than the gift of dwelling places, better than accepting guidance.[38]

On occasion the Buddha confronts the householder, Sigala, who is about to make offerings to the quarters of the earth and sky (the four directions, the nadir and the zenith). The Buddha then informs Sigala that the true worship of the quarters is the virtuous life:

Inasmuch, young householder, as the Ariyan disciple has put away the four vices in conduct — . . . slaughter of life, theft, lying, adultery . . . inasmuch as he does no evil actions from the four motives — . . . partiality, enmity, stupidity and fear . . . inasmuch as he does not pursue the six channels for dissipating wealth — . . . being addicted to intoxicating liquors, frequenting the streets at unseemly hours, haunting fairs, the being infatuated by gambling, associating with evil companions, the habit of idleness . . . he thus, avoiding these fourteen evil things, is a coverer of the six quarters.[39]

Sigala is instructed further, toward the perfection in generosity, to honor parents, teachers, wife, friends and companions, servants and working people, and the Bhikkhus. Ministering to the needs of these six types of persons is the true worship of the six quarters: as concerns parents, for example:

In five ways a child should minister to his parents as the eastern quarter: — Once supported by them I will now be their support; I will perform duties incumbent on them; I will keep up the lineage and tradition of my family; I will make myself worthy of my heritage.

In five ways parents thus ministered to, as the eastern quarter, by their child, show their love for him: —

they restrain him from vice, they exhort him to virtue, they train him to a profession, they contract a suitable marriage for him, and in due time they hand over his inheritance.[40]

Perfection of faith and of virtue is to be the central concern in the layman's observance four times each lunar month of the Uposatha. On these occasions he goes to the monastery, takes the threefold refuge, listens to the enlightening word of the Buddha, chanted and preached by the Bhikkhus, and commits himself for the day to eight precepts — in addition to the above-mentioned five: abstaining from food after noon until the next morning, abstaining from adorning his body or participating in inappropriate shows or sports, and abstaining from the use of comfortable beds or seats.

The layman's giving of good gifts is dependent upon his wealth. He is encouraged to labor for wealth:

> Housefather, there are these four kinds of bliss to be won by the householder . . . the bliss of ownership, the bliss of wealth, the bliss of debtlessness, the bliss of blamelessness . . .
>
> [bliss of ownership] . . . wealth acquired by energetic striving, amassed by strength of arm, won by sweat, lawful and lawfully gotten . . .
>
> [bliss of wealth] . . . by means of wealth acquired . . . (he) both enjoys his wealth and does meritorious deeds therewith . . .
>
> [bliss of debtlessness] . . . (he) owes no debt great or small to anyone . . .
>
> [bliss of blamelessness] . . . blameless action of body, speech and mind . . .[41]

Thus the layman pursues wealth by honest, hard work, without infraction of the precepts,[42] without taking unfair advantage of the wealth of others and with a view to good deeds as well as personal enjoyment. There are four conditions to his "advantage and happiness here on earth" — alertness, wariness, good company, and the even life: ". . . (by) whatsoever activity a clansman make his living . . . he is deft and tireless; gifted with an inquiring turn of mind into ways and means, he is able to arrange and carry out his job. This is called achievement in alertness." He is wary lest his wealth be diminished by theft, fire, flood, or relatives; he keeps companionship and intimacy with persons of like values and he ". . . while experiencing both gain and loss in wealth, continues his business serenely, not unduly elated or depressed. . . . This is called the even life."[43]

There are ten types of enjoyers of sense-pleasures — among them

> . . . he who seeks after wealth lawfully, not arbitrarily, and in so doing makes himself happy and cheerful, also shares his wealth with others, and further does meritorious deeds therewith, and yet makes use of his wealth without greed and longing, without infatuation, heedful of the danger and alive to his own salvation — of these ten this one is best and chief, topmost, highest, and supreme.[44]

". . . Riches gotten by work and zeal, gathered by the strength of the arm, earned by the sweat of the brow, justly obtained in a lawful way . . ." are to be used in five ways:

1. To provide material welfare to parents, wife, children, employees, and oneself
2. To provide the same for friends and companions
3. To keep one's goods safe from bad luck, fire and water, kings and robbers, enemies, and heirs
4. To make the five offerings to kin, guests, Petas (hungry ghosts), kings, and gods (Devas)
5. To make offerings to the Bhikkhus

. . . he institutes offerings, of lofty aim, celestial,
ripening to happiness, leading heavenward, for all those
recluses and godly men who abstain from pride and in-
dolence, who bear all things in patience and humility,
each mastering self, each calming self, each perfecting
self.[45]

The last of these uses of wealth is clearly the most important. It is the layman's first duty to provide the four requisites for those who have taken up the way of the monk:

Housefather, possessed of four things the Ariyan disciple has entered on the householder's path of duty, a
path which brings good repute and leads to the heaven
world. What are the four?

Herein, housefather, the Ariyan disciple waits upon the
Order of monks, he waits upon the Order of monks with
the offer of a robe, alms-food . . . lodging . . . requisites
and medicines for use in sickness. These are the four
things.[46]

The relative merit of an offering (a gift or charitable act)
depends upon the worth or merit of the giver and the recipient — the gift which is purified by a giver and a receiver who
are both pure is the best of all gifts; a gift to human beings
is of greater merit than a gift to lower animals; a gift to the
monk is second only to one given the Buddha himself.[47]

The layman who has moved skillfully to acquire wealth
without infraction of the precepts and has continually engaged in the five kinds of meritorious action gains "riches
through his industry," and high status in his society; he "dies
without anxiety," confident of rebirth in a happy state.[48]

I have enjoyed my wealth. Those serving me
And those dependent on me have escaped
From dangers. I have made the best of gifts,
Nay, done th' oblations five. The virtuous,

Composed, who live the good life, I've supported.
That aim the which to win householders wise
Should long for wealth, I've won. I've done a deed
Never to be regretted, — pondering thus
A mortal man in Ariyan dhamma firm
Is praised in this world, then in heaven rejoices.[49]

The Way of the King

Though himself a layman, the king, because he holds temporal power, should recognize unique responsibilities toward the Buddha-sasana. He is charged not only with keeping order in his state, protecting the people from each other and outside enemies, but is himself to be an example of purity, self-discipline, and charity for all men, a 'Wheel-turning (the Wheel of the Dhamma) Monarch':

> But what, sire, is this Ariyan duty of a Wheel-turning Monarch?
> This, dear son, that thou, leaning on the Norm (the Law of truth and righteousness) honouring, respecting and revering it, doing homage to it, hallowing it, being thyself a Norm [Dhamma]-banner, a Norm-signal, having the Norm as thy master, shouldst provide the right watch, ward, and protection for thine own folk, for the army, for the nobles, for vassals, for brahmins, and householders, for town and country dwellers, for the religious world, and for beasts and birds. Throughout thy kingdom let no wrongdoing prevail. And whosoever in thy kingdom is poor, to him let wealth be given.[50]

> . . . what a sovran or a minister of state shows homage to, or offers worship, to that will the rest of mankind, on the ground of the homage of so powerful a personage, show homage to and worship. . . .[51]

The 'Wheel-turning Monarch' conquers by the power of the Dhamma — as if a great Dhamma wheel had rolled on before him and prepared his way, his former enemies bow to him and receive instruction in the five precepts.[52]

In ancient times kingship was first established by popular election out of the concern of the people for the censure and punishment of wrongdoing. The Buddha addresses Vasettha (a disciple):

> Now those beings, Vasettha, gathered themselves together, and bewailed these things, saying: From our evil deeds, sirs, becoming manifest, inasmuch as stealing, censure, lying, punishment have become known, what if we were to select a certain being, who should be wrathful when indignation is right, who should censure that which should rightly be censured and should banish him who deserves to be banished? But we will give him in return a proportion of the rice.
>
> Then, Vasettha, those beings went to the being among them who was the handsomest, the best favoured, the most attractive, the most capable and said to him: Come now, good being, be indignant at that whereat one should rightly be indignant, censure that which should rightly be censured, banish him who deserves to be banished. And we will contribute to thee a proportion of our rice.
>
> And he consented, and did so, and they gave him a proportion of their rice.[53]

This king was called Maha Sammata ". . . since he was recognized (*sammata*) by the majority (*maha-jana*)". . .; he was called king (*raja*) ". . . since he promoted others' good (*ranjeti*) righteously and equitably. . . ."[54]

> . . . the sovran overlord gains the favour of the people by the four elements of popularity (liberality, affability, justice, and impartiality) . . .[55]

Like King Vessantara (the next to the last rebirth of the Buddha), the king should give of his wealth to all who are in need. Yet the king is not simply a "super" layman (setting example in keeping the precepts and giving good gifts); of all laymen, he alone is responsible for guiding and chastening the Bhikkhu-Sangha:

And when, dear son, in thy kingdom men of religious life, renouncing the carelessness arising from the intoxication of the senses, and devoted to forbearance and sympathy, each mastering self, each calming self, each perfecting self, shall come to thee from time to time, and question thee concerning what is good and what is bad, what is criminal and what is not, what is to be done and what left undone, what line of action will in the long run work for weal or for woe, thou shouldst hear what they have to say, and thou shouldst deter them from evil, and bid them take up what is good. This, dear son, is the Ariyan duty of a sovran of the world.[56]

A king possesses wealth and power because of his self-discipline and meritorious deeds in former lives:

Now there occurred . . . this thought to the Great King of Glory [Maha-Sudassana]: — "Of what previous character, now, may this be the fruit, of what previous character the result, that I am now so mighty and so great?"

"And then occurred . . . to the Great King of Glory this thought: — "Of three qualities is this the fruit, of three qualities the result, that I am now so mighty and so great, — that is to say, of giving, of self-conquest, and of self-control."[57]

Likewise, a king maintains and enhances his position now and in future lives by continued discipline and deeds of merit — Maha-Sudassana, in addition to performing deeds of merit, practiced meditation and entered the four raptures;[58] he practiced mindfulness of loving-kindness, compassion, sympathetic joy, and equanimity; and upon death, he was reborn in one of the happy Brahma-worlds.[59] So long as the king adheres to the Dhamma, so long will his kingdom prosper. Thus the word of the Buddha to the Vajjian rulers:

> So long, Ananda, as the Vajjians meet together in concord, and rise in concord, and carry out their undertakings in concord — so long as they enact nothing not already established, abrogate nothing that has been already enacted, and act in accordance with the ancient institutions of the Vajjians, as established in former days — so long as they honour and esteem and revere and support the Vajjian elders, and hold it a point of duty to hearken to their words — so long as no women or girls belonging to their clans are detained among them by force or abduction — so long as they honour and esteem and revere and support the Vajjian shrines in town or country, and allow not the proper offerings and rites, as formerly given and performed, to fall into desuetude — so long as the rightful protection, defense, and support shall be fully provided for the Arahants [accomplished Bhikkhus] among them, so that Arahants from a distance may enter the realm, and the Arahants therein may live at ease — so long may the Vajjians be expected not to decline, but to prosper.[60]

However, should the king think to go his own way, being remiss in his Dhamma-prescribed duties, the kingdom will suffer gradual deterioration. The king's failure to bestow wealth upon the poor will give rise to theft, theft to violence, violence to murder, murder to lying, lying to evil speaking, adultery, abusive and idle talk, covetousness and ill will, false opinions, incest, wanton greed, perverted lust, and finally the total lack of regard for the Dhamma and for the king.[61]

IV

Historical Development

THERAVADA BUDDHISTS of Southeast Asia adhere to a tradition crystallized and codified in large measure by the Bhikkhus of the Mahavihara (Great Monastery) of Ceylon between the third century B.C. and the fifth century A.D. It cannot be said with certainty when and how this tradition was first introduced into Southeast Asia. It appears that Ceylonese Buddhist influence, first in Burma and later in lower Thailand, begins only in the eleventh century A.D. It is not until the late twelfth century that an order of monks adhering to the Theravada tradition is established in Burma. The Thai officially recognize Theravada Buddhism in the mid-thirteenth century and the Khmer and Lao, in the early fourteenth century.

Ceylonese, Burmese, and Thai Buddhist chronicles[1] report that the Buddha himself visited points in Ceylon, Burma, and upper and lower Thailand during his lifetime. They further report that in the latter part of the third century B.C. "The Way of the Elders" was established in Southeast Asia by one or more monk-missions dispatched from India by a council of Bhikkhus under the patronage of King Asoka (269–232 B.C.).[2] Neither the Buddha-visits nor the Asokan missions can be substantiated from other sources. Archeological findings indicate the presence of a Hinayana

Buddhism in lower Thailand from the second century A.D.
and at Old Prome (central Burma) from ca. A.D. 500.
Hinayana Buddhism was prominently practiced in the Mon
kingdom of Dvaravati, encompassing a large portion of
present-day Thailand and Lower Burma and flourishing
from the sixth to the eleventh centuries A.D. Dvaravati
Buddhism was influenced from Amaravati (South India)
and possibly Ceylon as well. The Burmese, Thai, and Khmer
peoples were in turn influenced in Hinayana Buddhism
through contact with Mon culture.

Mahavihara Buddhism was established in Ceylon by
King Devanampiya Tissa in the latter half of the third century B.C. According to the Sinhalese (Ceylonese) chronicles
the Buddha visited Ceylon on three different occasions, pre-
paring the island for the coming of Buddhism and foretelling
its greatness there. In the course of these visits he terrorized
and sent away a mass of malevolent spirits (*yakkha*); he
preached to an assemblage of gods (*deva*); he settled a
dispute between two Naga ("snake") kings and 'converted'
many of their followers; and finally, he left his footprint on
Sumana Peak where he had earlier presented several of
his hairs to the Deva of the peak for enshrinement in a
thupa.[3] From the Buddha's death to the establishment under
King Devanampiya, Theravada Buddhism was reaffirmed
by three great councils of Bhikkhus the last of which it is
said dispatched missionary monks to various parts of the
world including Ceylon. The first of the councils met at
Rajagaha immediately following the death of the Buddha
and the Bhikkhus recited and codified the basic teachings
and discipline (Dhamma-Vinaya) of the master. The second
council met at Vesali one hundred years later and again
recited the teachings and the discipline in ruling against
certain aberrant practices of the Vajjian monks. This action,
it is suggested by the chroniclers, was the beginning of the
Theravada-Mahayana split and the division among the
monks became so pronounced by the mid-third century B.C.
that King Asoka himself urged a council (the third) to set-

tle differences and disrobe those Bhikkhus who would not adhere to the correct discipline and teachings. The council met at Asoka's capital, Pataliputta, in 247 B.C. under the leadership of the elder Bhikkhu, Mogaliputta Tissa, purified the Sangha, and clearly established the validity of the Theravada tradition.[4] Mogaliputta then directed the sending out of missionary monks:

> The thera Majjhantika he sent to Kasmira and Gandhara, the thera Mahadeva he sent to Mahisamandala. To Vanavasa he sent the thera named Rakkhita, and to Aparantaka the Yona named Dhammarakkhita; to Maharattha (he sent) the thera named Mahadhammarakkhita, but the thera Maharakkhita he sent into the country of the Yona. He sent the thera Majjhima to the Himalaya country, and to Suvannabhumi he sent the two theras Sona and Uttara. The great thera Mahinda, the theras Itthiya, Uttiya, Sambala and Bhaddasala his disciples, these five theras he sent forth with the charge: "Ye shall found in the lovely island of Lanka [Ceylon] the lovely religion of the Conquerer."[5]

The Dhamma was first preached to King Devanampiya by the monk Mahinda, a son of King Asoka. Becoming a lay devotee, King Devanampiya officially established "The Way of the Elders" and built a great monastery (the Mahavihara) at his capital, Anuradhapura, for the Bhikkhus ordained by Mahinda. A short time later a nun (*bhikkhuni*), Sanghamitta, the daughter of King Asoka, brought a branch of the Bodhi tree[6] to Ceylon and founded there an order of nuns. In spite of frequent warfare and periods of non-Buddhist rule, Buddhism enjoyed official support and considerable prosperity under most of the kings reigning at Anuradhapura from the third century B.C. to the tenth century A.D. Buddhist kings of the period competed with each other in building lavish monasteries and monuments and both Buddhist and non-Buddhist rulers paid due respect to the Sangha as a powerful support in controlling the people. In the latter part of the period the monks not only supported claimants to the throne but on occasion conferred kingship at the monastery. The Sangha came to depend upon the king to enforce its judgments on monks guilty of offenses against the discipline, and various of the kings intervened to settle inter-Sangha disputes. The Buddhist king came to be looked upon as a "wheel-turning" (*cakkavatti*) monarch and even a Bodhisatta (Future Buddha). In the fourth century A.D. a Buddha-tooth was brought to Ceylon from India and thereafter possession of this tooth was considered prerequisite to occupation of the throne. Mahavihara Buddhism did not always enjoy official support; it came to be rivaled by "Mahayana-leaning" groups of monks, and on more than one occasion the main monastery was destroyed by a king supporting a rival group or by Hindu invaders.[7] It was not until the twelfth century that the Sinhalese Sangha was united in adherence to the Mahavihara tradition.

In the latter part of the first century B.C., threatened by famine, official support for a non-Theravada tradition, laxity among the monks, and general political turmoil, Mahavihara monks gathered and committed the Dhamma and Vinaya to written form in the Pali language.[8] The Pali texts, considered authoritative in Southeast Asia, are read in the light of commentaries composed in Ceylon. Most of these commentaries are attributed to one Buddhaghosa, a Bhikkhu, who according to the chronicles came to Ceylon from northwest India around A.D. 400. Buddhaghosa summarized and interpreted the *Tipiṭaka* in his *Visuddhimagga* and wrote commentaries based on a large body of existing Sinhalese expositions.[9]

The Burmese and Thai chronicles, following the Sinhalese, submit that the Buddha visited not only Ceylon but also various points on the mainland of Southeast Asia. In Burma the Buddha preached at Lekaing village, left his footprint on Mount Saccabandha, and on Mount Hpo-u prophesied the coming greatness of Buddhism at this place.[10] According to the *Sāsanavaṃsa*, the Buddha gave special attention to the Sudhammapura (Thaton) area of Lower Burma, preaching there, leaving hair-relics, and finally, sending his disciple, Gavampati, to firmly establish the faith.[11] Both the *Sāsanavaṃsa* and the *Cāmadevīvaṃsa* note a visit of the Buddha to the Haribhunja country (northern Thailand). A Lao legend relates how the Buddha while wandering stopped at the site of the That Luang (a great Stupa in Vientiane) and foretold that the Emperor Asoka of India would build a monument on his spot and Buddhism would prosper here in years to come.[12]

As to the Bhikkhu-missions dispatched by Mogaliputta following the third council, Pannasami, the Burmese chronicler, argues that Vanavasa is Sirikhetta (Sriksetra) or Old Prome in Burma; Aparantaka is Burma, west of the Irrawaddy River; Maharattha is Siyama (Siam); the country of the Yona is the Haribhunja country (Shan states and northern Thailand); and that Suvannabhumi is Sudhammapura (Thaton) in southern Burma.[13] It is clear from other evidence, however, that all of these references except the last, Suvannabhumi, are to areas on the Indian subcontinent or to the northwest thereof. Critical historians agree with Pannasami that Suvannabhumi, "Land of Gold," refers to some portion of Southeast Asia but as to which portion there is no agreement. The Thai maintain that it refers to the Nakon Pathom area, southwest of Bangkok, where, in fact, archaeological findings indicate the presence of Hinayana Buddhism as early as the second century A.D. They also point out that certain of the names of places near Nakon Pathom such as U-tong and Supanburi have the same general meaning as Suvannabhumi.[14] The *Mahāvaṃsa* reports that in Suvannabhumi:

Many were the people who came unto the (three) refuges and the precepts of duty; sixty thousand were converted to the true faith. Three thousand five hundred sons of noble families received the pabbajja and one thousand five hundred daughters of noble families received it likewise. Thenceforth when a prince was born in the royal palace the kings gave to such the name Sonuttara.[15]

Wherever the location of Suvannabhumi, there is no evidence of the presence of Buddhism in Southeast Asia at this early date (247 B.C.). There is substantial evidence of the reign of King Asoka in India, in the main, the rock and pillar edicts which he had cut and erected throughout his domain. However, there is no reference in these edicts to any council of monks or to Bhikkhu-missions to surrounding countries, and scholars disagree as to the role of Asoka in the support and propagation of Buddhism. The chroniclers report that Asoka, formerly evil (Candasoka) but later devout (Dhammasoka),[16] was the ideal Buddhist monarch, purifier and preserver of the Sangha, builder of thousands (84,000) of monasteries and monuments, ruling according to the Buddhist ethic.[17] The edicts indicate that Asoka did, early in his reign, undergo a dramatic change of heart; that he eschewed violence; that he urged upon his ministers and people an ethic very much like that prescribed for the Theravada Buddhist laity; and that he patronized various religious institutions and traditions, among them those of Buddhism.[18]

Having established that Suvannabhumi and Sudhammapura (Thaton) were one and the same, the Burmese chroniclers assert further that the great Bhikkhu-scholar, Buddhaghosa, was from Thaton, not India and when he had completed his work in Ceylon he returned to Lower Burma with both *Tipitaka* and commentaries.[19] The chroniclers' continued reference to Thaton as the ancient center of Theravada Buddhism is probably an attempt to press backward from the well-documented fact that in the eleventh century A.D. King Anoratha and his general Kyanzittha established a Hinayana Buddhism at Pagan (central Burma) as the result of conquests in Lower Burma. There is evidence of the presence of Hinayana Buddhism at old Prome (central Burma), the center of the kingdom of Sriksetra, from ca. A.D. 500, and archaeologists have recently established that a Hinayana Buddhism flourished from the sixth to the eleventh centuries in the Mon kingdom of Dvaravati, encompassing a large portion of present-day Thailand and Lower Burma and having its capital at Nakon Pathom, thirty miles southwest of Bangkok. The remains of Dvaravati reveal that its Hinayana Buddhism was influenced from Amaravati (South India), a center of both Hinayana and Mahayana Buddhism flourishing in the third century A.D. In the eleventh century Dvaravati fell to the Burmese in the West and to the Khmer in the East, and by the middle of the thirteenth century the Thai came into control in the North. Nonetheless, Mon-Buddhist culture prevailed. According to the chronicles, Anoratha (1044–77) influenced by a Mon Bhikkhu, Shin Arahan, from Thaton conquered Thaton[20] in 1057 in order to gain possession of Pali texts and Bhikkhus with which to establish Hinayana Buddhism at Pagan. Anoratha's conquest occasions Mon-culture influence at Pagan and the establishment of Hinayana Buddhism at the expense of the Tantric Mahayanism then popular in the area. David Luce has recently argued that it was Anoratha's general, Kyanzittha [who later (1084–1113) ruled at Pagan], rather than Anoratha, who was the key figure in the Hinayana establishment and the spread of Mon culture.[21] Archaeologists allow that the Buddhism of Dvaravati may have been influenced from Ceylon as well as South India, but the first clear evidence of Sinhalese influence in Southeast Asia comes from the Anoratha-Kyanzittha period. Sinhalese Buddhism had suffered severe decline in the eleventh century due largely to the conquest of Ceylon by the Hindu Cholas of South India. In his struggle to drive out the Cholas and reestablish the Sinhalese Sangha, King Vijayabahu I (1070–1110) requested aid from Anoratha. Burmese monks, having gone to Ceylon to revive the Sinhalese Sangha, returned to Burma with Pali texts and initiated a long-term interaction between the two countries. Under Parakramabahu I (1153–86) and his successors in the twelfth and thirteenth centuries, Sinhalese Buddhism enjoyed great prosperity, and numerous monks from the Southeast Asian mainland traveled to Ceylon for ordination and education. The Mon monk, Chapata, having spent ten years in the island, returned to Burma in 1190 to found a Sinhalese Sangha rivaling the older ordination line introduced from Thaton. Kings Narapati (1443–68) and Thihathura (1469–81), ruling from Ava (Burma), patronized the Temple of the Tooth in Kandy, providing amenities there for Burmese monks on pilgrimage.[22] King Bayinnaung (1551–81) sent offerings to Kandy and upon request received a bride and a Buddha-tooth from the King of Colombo.

Burmese Buddhists had occasion to repay their debt to Ceylon in the nineteenth century as the Sinhalese sought new ordination lines from Burma. The Amarapura Nikaya and the Ramanna Nikaya, two of the three orders within the Ceylonese Sangha today, were founded from Burma in 1803 and 1863, respectively.[23] The third and largest of the three orders of the Ceylonese Sangha, the Siam Nikaya, was (as the name indicates) founded from Thailand in the eighteenth century. King Boromokot of Ayut'ia (1733–57) dispatched a group of Thai Bhikkhus to Ceylon in 1753 at the request of King Kirtisiri of Kandy. The mission remained in Ceylon for three years, ordaining 700 Bhikkhus and 3,000 novices.[24]

The Thai peoples, the ancestors of the Shan of Burma and the Lao as well as the present-day Thai, gradually moved southward into the Irrawaddy and Menam River basins from Yunnan Province, China, beginning in the eighth century A.D. The Lan Na Thai of northern Thailand and those who settled farther south along the Menam River first came under the influence of Hinayana Buddhism through contact with Mon civilization. The Lan Na Thai chronicles record that Queen Camadevi of Lopburi (central Thailand) brought Hinayana Buddhism to the north (Haribhunja or Lamphun) in the seventh century A.D.[25] The conquests of Anoratha in the upper Irrawaddy basin and northern Thailand brought Hinayana Buddhism to the Shan and reinforced that already known among the Lan Na. Under Khmer influence to the middle of the thirteenth century, the Thai who settled in the Menam River basin were introduced to Brahmanism and Mahayana Buddhism as well as the Mon Hinayana. When they rose to power with the decline of the power of Angkor, Sinhalese Buddhism was enjoying great popularity in Lower Thailand. The *Jinakālamālinī* records that a now famous Sinhalese Buddha-image, the Phra Buddha Sihing, was brought to Sukhodaya in A.D. 1256.[26] The third king of Sukhodaya, Rama Khamhaeng (1275–1317), invited a famous Bhikkhu from Nakon Sri Dhammaraj (southern Thailand) to his court and thereafter officially established Sinhalese Theravada Buddhism. A rock inscription dated 1292 records that:

> King Rama Khamhaeng, sovereign of this Muang Sukhothai, [Sukhodaya] as well as the princes and princesses, men as well as women, nobles and chiefs, all without exception, without distinction of rank or sex, devoutly practice the religion of the Buddha and observe the precepts during the period of retreat during the rainy season. At the end of the rainy season, the ceremonies of the Kathin take place and last a month.[27]

From Sukhodaya, Sinhalese Buddhist traditions were introduced among the Lan Na Thai who had established a kingdom at Chiengmai to the north. King Kuna of Chiengmai (1355–85) established the Sinhalese tradition under the guidance of a high-ranking Ceylon-ordained Mon Bhikkhu, Mahasami Sangharaj Sumana, who had been a favorite of King Dhammaraja ("Lord of the Dhamma") Lu T'ai of Sukhodaya (1347–61).

The Buddhist Thai kings of Sukhodaya adopted certain of the Brahmanistic practices of the kings of Angkor and in turn, from the Ayut'ia period to the nineteenth century, the Thai influenced the practice of Theravada Buddhism among the Khmer. It appears, however, that as with the Burmese and the Thai, it was the Mon who introduced the Khmer to Theravada Buddhism. The rulers of ancient Funan (first to the sixth century A.D.) and Chenla (sixth to the eighth centuries), kingdoms centered in the area of present-day Cambodia, and the kings of Angkor to ca. A.D. 1300 patronized Brahmanism, Hinduism, and Mahayana Buddhism. Jayavarman VII, ruling at Angkor from 1181 to 1200, patronized Mahayana Buddhism; yet his son, Tamalinda, was one of the monks who accompanied the Mon Bhikkhu, Chapata, to Ceylon in 1180.[28] We have no further evidence of the activities of Tamalinda, but the account of Chou Ta-kuan, a Chinese envoy to the court of Angkor in 1295, indicates that Hinayana (and possibly the Sinhalese Theravada) Buddhism was prominently practiced at that time:

> The Buddhist monks (ch'u-ku) shave the head, wear yellow robes, bare the right shoulder, knot a strip of yellow cloth round the waist and go bare-foot. Their temples, which are often roofed with tile, contain only one statue, closely resembling the Buddha Sakyamuni, which is called Po-lai (= Prah). . . . There are no bells, no drums, no cymbals, no banners. The food of the bonzes is universally fish or meat, which is also set as an offering before the Buddhas; but no wine may be drunk. They content themselves with one meal a day, which is partaken of at the home of a patron, no cooking being done in the monasteries. . . . To certain monks is given the right to use palanquins with golden shafts and parasols with gold or silver handles. These men are consulted by the King in matters of serious import. There are no Buddhist nuns.
> Worship of the Buddha is universal.[29]

The oldest Cambodian inscription in the Pali language dates from 1309, and it appears that Sinhalese Buddhism was first officially patronized by Jayavarman Paramesvara who began to rule at Angkor in 1327. In 1353, Fa Ngum, the son-in-law of Jayavarman Paramesvara, established the kingdom of Lan Chang over the Lao people in the upper Mekong area (the present-day Luang Prabang area) and a short time later requested his former monk-preceptor at Angkor to bring texts and Bhikkhus to his capital with which to establish Theravada Buddhism. The Bhikkhu-mission from Angkor brought with them the now famous Phra Bang Buddha-image which, according to tradition, originated in Ceylon and after which Fa Ngum's capital was later named.[30]

Thus it is that by the mid-fourteenth century, Sinhalese Theravada Buddhism became well established all across the area of its present-day influence. The frequent warfare between the Thai, Burmese, Khmer, and Lao from the fourteenth through the early nineteenth centuries appears to have had little negative effect on the common faith of all parties. Once established, the Bhikkhu-ordination line of the various Southeast Asian kingdoms never lapsed as it did more than once in the mother country, Ceylon, and, in fact, it may be argued that the Sanghas of Thailand, Laos, and Cambodia are today stronger than that of Ceylon due largely to continuous royal patronage.

The chronicles and inscriptions relating the later history of Theravada Buddhism in Southeast Asia are most interesting as they reveal the piety of king and court and the developing relationship between king and Sangha, the practice in both matters being quite in keeping with the classical ideal of Buddhist kingship. Numerous Theravada kings styled themselves 'Dhammaraja' ("Lord of the Dhamma") and some like Alaungpaya (literally, "embryo-Buddha") and Bodawpaya of Burma and Taksin of Thailand considered themselves 'Future-Buddhas'. The piety of the Theravada kings is testified to by the lavish monasteries and burial monuments which they constructed to the Buddha and to themselves — witness the Ananda Pagoda of Kyanzittha at

Pagan, the Wat Umong of King Kuna at Chiengmai, with its elaborate vaults and tunnels made to order for a favorite monk's meditations;[31] and the That Luang and Pra Keo temples of Sethathirath (1548–70) at Vientiane, the latter built for the fabulous Emerald Buddha. King Mindon Min (1852–77) topped the Shwe Dagon Pagoda at Rangoon with an umbrella (*hti*) studded with jewels then worth £ 62,000.[32] In more recent times, not king but prime minister, U Nu had a great cave constructed for the Sixth Council of Bhikkhus at a cost of over $2,000,000.[33] In accordance with the Theravada ideal, Buddhist kings and their subjects believed that kingly power was based on merit — the merit of former lives and the merit of piety in the present life. As clearly expressed in a 1918 address to the king of Thailand by the Supreme Patriarch (Sangharaja), the king's acts of piety merit not only himself but the people and the guardian spirits of the kingdom.[34] The piety of the king also takes the form of exhortations to the people concerning the practice of Buddhism — Kings Potisarat (1520–47) of Laos[35] and Rama I (1782–1809) of Thailand are noted for their decrees subordinating local spirit-cults to the way of the Buddha. Rama I commanded the people not to honor the spirits (*phii*) and gods (*devas*) more highly than they honor the three gems (Buddha, Dhamma, Sangha) and not to offer bloody sacrifices to spirits —

> . . . men should perform meritorious acts by liberality and good conduct and dedicate the result of it if they like to the tutelary or other spirits.[36]

A significant number of the kings of Buddhist Southeast Asia were monks prior to taking the throne and some were learned in the Pali texts. King Lu T'ai of Sukhodaya composed a treatise on cosmology, the *Traibhūmikathā*, and upon giving up his throne became a monk.[37] Rama IV of Thailand (1850–68) spent twenty-seven years as a monk, becoming an expert in the Pali texts, prior to becoming king.

As was the case with King Asoka of India (according to traditional accounts) and a number of the Buddhist kings of Ceylon, many of the kings of Theravada Southeast Asia are noted for their actions as 'Protector and Purifier' of the Sangha. Among the kings of Burma, King Dammazedi of Pegu (1472–92), a former monk in the Sinhalese ordination line, dispatched a large group of Bhikkhus to Ceylon in 1476 for reordination. His intent was to unify the Burmese Sangha[38] and enforce stricter adherence to the discipline by insisting that all Bhikkhus belong to one jurisdiction which came to be known as the Kalyani[39] Sima. King Bodawpaya of Burma, ruling from Amarapura from 1782 to 1819, settled by decree a long-standing Sangha dispute over the proper wearing of the robe.[40] Bodawpaya is also credited with a further unifying of the Sangha by the appointment of eight elder Bhikkhus as Sangharajas to serve under the king's monk-preceptor, the Mahasangharaja, in the administration of the monastic order.[41] King Mindon Min (1852–77) added to this administrative structure a council of elder Bhikkhus (the Thudhamma Council) to try errant monks for offenses against the state. Mindon is noted for his consultations with monks concerning civil affairs such as the appointment of village officials; but he is most renowned among the kings of Burma for having convoked a great council of Bhikkhus at Mandalay in 1871 for the revision of the Pali texts.[42] Following the council he had the 'purified' texts inscribed on stone tablets and enshrined in Stupas. Prime Minister U Nu spearheaded the revival of Buddhism in independent Burma by convoking the Sixth Great Buddhist Council at Rangoon in 1954. In session for two years, the gathering of Bhikkhus, following tradition, recited the entire *Tipiṭaka*. The council was recognized by the Sanghas of the other Theravada countries, and leading monks from Ceylon, Thailand, Laos, and Cambodia took part. U Nu was elected in 1960 on a platform urging the establishment of Theravada Buddhism as the state religion of Burma. The bills[43] accomplishing this establishment were passed in August and September of 1961.

Among Thai rulers, Rama I, founder of the Cakri dynasty ruling from Bangkok, most notably exercised his prerogative to protect and reform the Sangha. Between 1782 and 1801, he issued no less than ten edicts pertaining to the activities of the Bhikkhus. Herein he emphasized the necessity of the temporal and spiritual powers working together for the good of the Buddha-sasana and pointed up the duty of a Buddhist king to cleanse the Sangha when needful, sighting as examples King Ajatasatthu of India (according to the chronicles the caller of the first council of Bhikkhus) and King Parakramabahu of Ceylon. The edicts essentially command the Bhikkhus to faithfully preach the Dhamma and keep the Patimokkha discipline. Edicts III and IV require all monks to carry identification papers; Edict V specifies additional penalties for monks who are found guilty of *parajika* crimes[44] and disrobed;[45] Edict X indicates that the king has had one hundred and twenty-eight monks, found guilty of offense, disrobed and sentenced to hard labor.[46] In 1788, Rama I called a council of Thai Bhikkhus to revise and collate the Pali scriptures. Recognizing the three Indian councils, four councils in Ceylon,[47] and one at Chiengmai (under King Tiloka in the fifteenth century), he designated his council the ninth from the death of the Buddha. On the same order as the monk-consultations undertaken by King Mindon, Rama I and his successors issued a number of Royal Interrogations soliciting the views of the elder monks on civil affairs. Rama III, for example, inquired as to whether the imposition of dues and taxes on fishery and alcoholic beverages was not unethical by appearing to condone such immoral activities. The reply of the clergy was that these dues and taxes were to be understood as fines for offenses.[48] King Rama IV (Mongkut) of Thailand, ruling at Bangkok from 1850 to 1868, encouraged purity in the Sangha from within rather than as a result of royal decrees. As a monk he founded in 1873 a new order, the Dhammayutika, emphasizing strict adherence to the Vinaya and encouraging high learning among the Bhikkhus, and as king he supported this order.

Rama IV's successor, Chulalongkorn (1868–1910), appointed Mongkut's son Vajiranana as Supreme Patriarch (Sangharaja) of the Thai Sangha and with his assistance furthered the welfare of the Sangha by founding two Bhikku-seminaries at Bangkok, the Mahadhatu Rajavidyalaya (1890) and the Mahamakuta Rajavidyalaya (1893). These centers of higher education for the Bhikkhus have since played a major role in "modernizing" the Thai Sangha.[49]

The significant features of the history of Theravada Buddhism in Southeast Asia as revealed by chronicles and inscriptions are the long-term official status of the faith and the close working relationship between government and the Bhikkhu-Sangha, a relationship in which government patronized, consulted with, and controlled the Sangha and the Sangha provided a liaison between government and the people. These matters of history bear not only on the present status and role of Buddhism in Southeast Asia, but also upon its potential for the future.

PART II
The Practice of Buddhism

V

The Way of the Monk

In five ways should the clansman minister to recluses and brahmins as the zenith: — by affection
in act and speech and mind; by keeping open house
to them, by supplying their temporal needs.

Thus ministered to as the zenith, recluses and
brahmins show their love for the clansman in six
ways: — they restrain him from evil, they exhort
him to good, they love him with kindly thoughts;
they teach him what he has not heard, they correct
and purify what he has heard, they reveal to him
the way to heaven.[1]

THE PRACTICE of Theravada Buddhism in Southeast Asia
is in basic general accord with the prescriptions of the Pali
texts and the practical formulations of the Asokan Age and
early Sinhalese Theravada. The various kinds and conditions
of men express their refuge in the Buddha, Dhamma, and
Sangha according to their individual capacity and circumstances. There is great variety in the practice of Buddhism.
However, in a society and particularly in a Buddhist society,
the individual must exist and seek to enhance his own well-
being in relationship to others. Basic patterns of behavior —

customs, rituals, and organizations — have evolved in terms of which most Buddhists adhere to the Buddhist way, and, from one country to another in the Theravada tradition, these patterns are fundamentally the same.

The ideal society is one in which there is the greatest possible freedom and respect for the individual with regard to cultivation of compassion and wisdom; it is

> a non-coercive, non-authoritarian, democratic society where leadership comes only from good moral character and spiritual insight; where everyone confesses his sins to his brother; where all goods are held in common possession and every one, high or low, eats and dresses alike. It is an order of society which has no political ambitions within the nation, and in whose ranks there is no striving for leadership.[2]

This society is most closely approximated by the Bhikkhu-Sangha, the order of monks. Consequently, in the eyes of the laity, the monk is completely set apart from the rest of men, even from the king. A man joining this order is ritually cleansed and given a new name. This radical distinction between monk and nonmonk makes it possible and necessary to distinguish Buddhist patterns of life in terms of the way of the monk and the way of the laity.

We must bear in mind in doing so, however, that any male may apply for admission to the Bhikkhu-Sangha, that (providing he adheres to the discipline) he may remain in the order for as long or as short a time as he wishes, and leave again not only without stigma but with enhanced status as a layman. In fact, in all of the Theravada societies of Southeast Asia a great many men do apply and are admitted to the Bhikkhu-Sangha — it has become custom for the young man, if at all possible, to engage in the monastic life prior to marriage and the assumption of adult responsibility in the larger society. In a lifetime the status and role of an individual male may (and very often does) significantly change several times. There is constant interchange of persons between the Bhikkhu-way and the lay way. Further, we must bear in mind that the Bhikkhu-way, albeit the best way, is not the only 'true' Buddhism. The Bhikkhu through keeping the precepts, study, meditation, and compassionate service cultivates selflessness: — loving-kindness, compassion, sympathetic joy, and equanimity. The layman cultivates the same selflessness through keeping some of the precepts and through meritorious deeds with reference to the monk and the larger society. Even the layman's struggle with the malevolent spirit-forces which play upon his existence 'in the world' is carried on in the context of Buddhist values.

Winston King, in his discussion of "Buddhism: High, Low and Medium"[3] in Burma, suggests that the several patterns of adherence to the Buddhist way may be placed on a continuum, a kind of winding mountain path, from 'folk religion' at the base to 'Nibbana' at the summit. 'Pagoda religion', 'scriptural orthodoxy', 'the Sangha', 'meditation', and 'Buddhahood' fall in between. Such an upward- and inward-moving spiral suggests "the quality of fluidity and progression from one 'level' or 'stage' to another which is present in the living Buddhist structure."[4]

The great value of this schema lies in pointing up the fact that various levels of awareness and activity are functional within the one Buddhist-defined framework. This holds in all of the Southeast Asian Theravada societies. The schema has two limitations, however. First, it does not suggest enough 'fluidity'. In the daily and special practices of the layman propitiating spirit-forces (folk religion), offering candles, incense, and flowers before the Buddha-image (pagoda religion), keeping the precepts, feeding the Bhikkhus, listening to sermons, etc. (scriptural orthodoxy), and meditation (especially in Burma), all play a part. The meditating Bhikkhu pressing toward Buddhahood and Nibbana is, in one way or another, an agent in folk and pagoda Buddhism, and this is quite in accord with scriptural orthodoxy. The monk as well as the layman functions at several 'levels' at the same time. The second limitation of King's schema is that it places all Buddhists as pursuing the same goals when in actual practice they do not. For the great majority of Buddhists, even many of those who join the Bhikkhu-Sangha, Buddhahood and Nibbana are so far removed as not to be functional goals. The functional goal-orientations of the majority are high status and prosperity in this life and a more desirable rebirth beyond this life — the two goals being sides of the same coin.

As we proceed to discuss the many facets of the Buddhist way, we must remember that the 'real-life' is a symphony in which each theme is related in some way to every other theme and the beauty and strength of the whole lies in harmonious interaction. The individual pursuits are valued to the extent to which they are mutually supportive.

The Status of the Monk

Walking righteously is the Exalted One's Order of Disciples, walking uprightly, walking in the right path, walking dutifuly is the Exalted One's Order of Disciples. . . . That is the Exalted One's Order of Disciples. Worthy of honour are they, worthy of reverence, worthy of offerings, worthy of salutations with clasped hands, a field of merit unsurpassed for the world.[5]

It is difficult, if not impossible, for the nonnative of mainland Southeast Asia to appreciate the unique status of the monk in his society. Ordination to the monastic life marks the birth of a new being, an asexual being who must henceforth (as long as he remains a monk) be addressed or spoken about in a specially honorific language:

Ordinary laymen "eat rice," "smoke cheroots," or "drink tea"; monks performing these same actions are said to "honor" or "glorify the alms food," "honor the cheroot," etc. The laity "walks" or "sleeps" but monks "proceed," "remain dormant," or "in a state of repose."[6]

If he is addressed by name, even by family and friends, it is the formal name conferred upon him at ordination. In the presence of laymen the monk sits on a raised seat. The layman addressing the monk or making offerings to him must bow with clasped hands and sitting in the presence of the monk must keep his feet beneath his body and pointed away from the superior.[7] The monk community largely follows its own law, living under the prescriptions of the Vinaya texts of the Pali Canon. Monks accused of acts considered criminal by civil law must first be tried under a Bhikkhu-court and can be prosecuted by civil authority only after having been defrocked.

> The Laotian has given himself body and soul to the Good Law of which the monks are the representatives. As an image of the Buddha, the monk is respected and revered; everyone prostrates before him and no one suspects his good faith. No one dares to accuse nor even criticize him, since none of us has any idea of the extent of his knowledge.
>
> The monks are the masters and the inhabitants listen to them.[8]

The Burmese most frequently refer to the monk as '*pon-gyi*' (" 'Great Glory' ").

> The Burman demands from the monk . . . that he should live as becomes a follower of the great teacher. And because he does so live the Burman reverences him beyond all others. The king is feared, the wise man admired, perhaps envied, the rich man is respected, but the monk is honoured and loved. There is no one beside him in the heart of the people. If you would know what a Burman would be, see what a monk is: that is his ideal.[9]

There are over 600,000 Theravada monks (Bhikkhus and novices) residing in some 45,000 monasteries in the countries of mainland Southeast Asia: 260,000 in 23,700 wats[10] in Thailand, 250,000 in 17,000 kyaungs[11] in Burma, 93,000 in 2,850 wats in Cambodia, and 17,000 in 1,869 wats in Laos.[12] Even where these numbers are recent and fairly accurate, however (as in the case of those for Thailand), they should not be taken as indications of long-term membership in the Bhikkhu-Sangha. The great majority of those who enter the monastic order in any one year remain only a few months, usually the three months of the rainy-season retreat (Vassa). Less than 40 percent of those who become Bhikkhus or novices remain in the order for life. Such a large turnover does not signify lack of popular support for the way of the monk. In Theravada Southeast Asia joining the order for a time (however short) is the proper and preferred means of achieving recognition as a mature male and of repaying one's parents for the care they have given throughout childhood.[13] Being ordained to the order may also be the means to an education, otherwise unobtainable. In Burma almost every Buddhist male will spend some period of his life in the monastic order.[14] Throughout Theravada Southeast Asia there are many villages in which 75 to 85 percent of the male population over twenty years of age are or have been monks.[15]

Ordination

Undertaking the full discipline of the Bhikkhu-way requires a twofold ordination: first, the novitiate ordination (Pali: pabbajja); later, the Bhikkhu ordination (upasampada). One may receive the novitiate ordination at any age (usually ten years and over) but he cannot be ordained a Bhikkhu before the age of twenty. A young man ordained a Bhikkhu at age twenty may have had a lengthy association with the monastery in which he is ordained and the monks who ordain him. Patterns vary from one village and country to another. For example, in Laos an elder monk is consulted on the occasion of the naming of a child. The monk 'blesses' the child, perhaps hanging an especially prepared amulet around his neck for protection against evil spirits. If it is a male child, from that day forward he 'belongs to' or 'is under the care of' the monk. If the desires of the parents and the monk are fulfilled, the boy will later go to live in the monastery serving as a 'temple boy', receive his basic education under the tutelage of the monk, and be ordained as a novice and finally as a Bhikkhu under the same monk, his *khru* (guru) or master and teacher.[16] Throughout Theravada Southeast Asia it is customary for boys to serve as 'temple boys' assimilating something of Buddhist values while assisting the monk in receiving food and maintaining the monastery buildings and compound.[17] While government school systems are now in operation throughout the area, a great many children still receive their basic education under the monks at the monastery.[18]

Ordination is one of the most important occasions of village life. The entire village participates in the affair and at considerable expense of time and money[19] to the boy's parents and sponsor.[20] Very often, especially in Burma, more than one young man is ordained at the same time. A cooperative effort of several families may serve to reduce the expense to each of the families involved or it may simply provide the means for an even more lavish celebration. In recent times some Theravada laymen have formed associations (merit-societies) for free assistance to those undertaking an ordination or another of the elaborate celebrations of the Buddhist way.

Even though a man may be ordained a novice at any age, the preferred age is ten to eighteen years, and in fact, the great majority who become novices do so before the age of twenty. Novitiate ordination has come to function as a rite-of-passage from youth to adult status and thus ideally occurs at or near the attainment of puberty. In fact, we may say this ritual is a celebration of male fertility.

There are several preparatory rituals associated with the novitiate ordination varying in form from country to country and village to village but everywhere intended to accomplish the same ends. The parents of the boy may first consult an astrologer to set an auspicious date for the ritual in harmony with the ordinand's horoscope. On the day before and the day of the ordination parents, sponsor, and friends perform rituals in the home or in a pavilion especially constructed for the occasion to ensure the welfare of the candidate and at the same time to direct the 'power' generated by an ordination toward ensuring plentiful rain and fertility of the soil. The latter goal may seem extraordinary but is actually quite appropriate.

One who is to be ordained a novice is called a *naga* ("snake" or "serpent"). The name recalls an episode in the life of the Buddha wherein a *naga*, desirous of following the Master, assumed human form and gained ordination to the monastic life. Upon discovery of the true nature of the *'naga*-monk' the Buddha ordered the serpent to leave the Sangha but promised that he would be remembered on each occasion of ordination thereafter.[21] In the mythology of Indian Buddhism (and also Hinduism) the *naga*, in particular the *naga*-king, has his abode in the water thereby ruling over waters and has power over fertility in man and in the soil.[22] Given the association of the candidate for ordination with the *naga*, we must also note that the preferred time of year for ordination (especially for the large number who take up monkhood for the short term) is just prior to the rainy season. As the elder monks are confined to their monasteries during the Rain Retreat the novice is most likely to receive proper guidance and intensive instruction during this period.

On the night before the day of ordination Cambodian laymen and monks gather to call the *naga*-spirits and to make an offering to King (Krong) Pali, the *naga*-lord of water and soil. They also blacken the teeth (or symbolically blacken by scraping) of the candidate-*naga* by way of protecting him against evil spirits and assuring that he will remain in his human form.[23] In Burma on the day of ordination, members of the procession escorting the candidate-*naga* to the monastery call out for rain and fertility of the soil.[24] In Thailand and Laos the same association of the candidate-*naga* and fertility appears to be made but the rituals for rain (such as the Lao Boun Bang Fay) are not so obviously linked to ordination. To ensure the welfare of the candidate, Thai, Lao, and Khmer Buddhists and Shan Buddhists of Burma perform a *bai si*[25] or *sukhwan* ("calling the vital spirits") ceremony preparatory to ordination. The '*khwan*' is that which animates a person's body and mind; it tends to 'wander' and such wanderings are seen to account for physical and mental instability. Therefore, at all of the important transitional points of personal and communal life, and especially ordination, it is important that the vital spirits are 'collected' and 'sealed' in the body. The *sukhwan* ritual calls the *khwan,* offering them an elaborately arranged bowl of conical-shaped leaves bearing rice balls (*bai si*). The *khwan* are then sealed in the candidate's body by family and friends tying cotton threads around his wrist. Such a ritual is the vehicle for communal affirmation of support and well-wishing to the candidate at a very important moment in his life and the life of the entire community.

As a further means of ensuring the well-being of the ordination candidate Theravada Buddhists everywhere propitiate the guardian spirits of the household, family, and village. For example, in connection with the Burmese novitiate ordination (*shinbyu*), offerings are made to Min Mahagiri, the household spirit (*nat*), to the hereditary *nats* on the mother's and father's side of the family (*mizaing-hpazaing nats*), and the candidate is 'shown' to the village guardian *nat* at his shrine.[26]

> Because of the elaborateness of the ceremony and the fact that the children [the candidates] are the center of attention, parents fear the wrath of the nats whose envy is so easily aroused. . . . The *beiktheik hsaya,* master of

ceremonies hired for the occasion, ties a white thread in the children's hair, asking that the nats protect them.[27]

The major rituals of the day of ordination recall the Great Renunciation of Prince Gotama. Dressed in princely attire the ordinand is processed around the village and to the ordination hall riding on a horse or elephant or on the shoulders of a friend.[28] The procession is led by a host of young people masquerading as the 'army of Mara' seeking to deter the 'prince' from his renunciation. Very likely these young people are in fact the ordinand's peers and the life they enjoy is a temptation he must resist. Sponsor, parents, family, and friends also accompany the prince bearing the robes and alms-bowl he will shortly take up, and bearing the gifts for the monks who preside at the ceremony.[29] Having reached the ordination hall of the monastery or a pavilion erected for the occasion, the procession circles the hall three times (honoring the three gems: Buddha, Dhamma, Sangha) and presents the candidate at the door of the sanctuary. The 'host of Mara' makes one last (playful) effort to hold the 'prince' back and then permits him to present himself before the waiting monks. After the candidate has bowed before the Bhikkhus and requested admission to the order, the presiding monk asks him to designate his spiritual guide — the monk who will assist in the ordination and take primary responsibility for the novice in the days to come. The guide then admonishes the candidate that he is expected to adhere strictly to the rules of the monastic life. The candidate offers his robes and alms-bowl to the presiding monk and receives them back with instructions to withdraw and change clothing. If his head has not already been shaved this is now attended to and he may (especially in Burma) receive a ritual bath symbolically cleansing him of lay-life stains and warding off evil spirits. Upon return to the sanctuary the ordinand recites the ten precepts, vowing to abstain from: killing; stealing; sexual misconduct; lying;

drinking fermented beverages; eating at forbidden times; dancing, music, and shows; adorning the body with flowers, perfume, or ointments; sleeping on a high or wide bed; receiving money.[30] The candidate then does obeisance to his spiritual guide and this concludes the formal ceremony. The newly ordained novice leads the laity in presenting gifts and food-offerings to the gathered monks and, as with every merit-making ceremony, water is poured into a bowl or on the ground symbolically conveying the merit to all beings. In this context, the water is first poured on the novice and then on the ground by the novice.

The ordination-hall ceremony for the Bhikkhu ordination follows the same order as that for the novitiate ordination through the taking of the ten precepts. Then the ordinand is thoroughly questioned as to such things as whether he has the consent of his parents or wife (as the case may be), whether he is in good health, free from debt, and indeed a human being (not a spirit or animal). If the candidate has answered questioning satisfactorily and there are no objections voiced by the gathered monks, he is duly admitted to the order. The Bhikkhus then retire to recite privately the 227 rules and regulations of the full monastic life (the Patimokkha of the Vinaya texts) after which they return to the ordination hall to receive gifts and food-offerings. Thus, the Bhikkhu is committed to a more rigorous discipline than the novice, and we shall see this fact reflected in the kinds of activity in which each may engage.

There is a profound sense in which ordination signifies death and rebirth for the candidate. He gives up family and friends, all former associations, leaves off his old clothes, is shaved and ritually bathed, and finally receives a new name, the only name he will have as long as he remains a monk.[31]

The Education of the Monk

The length of time young men remain in the monastic order after ordination varies from a few days to a lifetime, and depends upon the circumstances under which they joined the order and whether or not they find the monastic life an agreeable one. Once having been ordained the ideal would be to pursue the Bhikkhu-way for a lifetime. Very few are able to commit themselves to this, and very many in fact spend only one rainy season as a novice, never becoming a Bhikkhu. The Thai government encourages this pattern by granting one rainy season's paid leave to civil servants who wish to be ordained. The Burmese encourage their young men to spend a minimum of three rainy seasons in the order — one for merit to the mother, one for merit to the father, and one for merit to the novice himself. There is an increasing tendency among urban Burmese Buddhists, however, to 'shinbyu' their sons at a very early age (as early as five years), and commit them to the monastery for only a few days — thus making the novitiate ordination purely a social formality.[32] This tendency is not peculiar to Burma, but in Thailand, Laos, and Cambodia, parent and child are likely to view ordination as more than a formality if for no other reason than that a bright young man may get a relatively good secondary and/or higher education as a monk. It is also relevant that there is greater merit in Bhikkhu ordination than in the novitiate ordination, and one who pursues his secondary and perhaps even higher education as a monk can achieve the Bhikkhu ordination before returning to lay life. In all of the Theravada countries of Southeast Asia a man may enter the monastic order and leave again more than once.[33] It is customary for a male of the family to become a monk for a few days upon the death of a relative transferring the merit to the deceased.

The short-term (one rainy season) novice concentrates on personal discipline, learning the basic teachings of the Buddha, and memorizing a few Pali texts to be recited in ritual. The longer-term monk is expected to study thoroughly the Dhamma, the monastic discipline (Vinaya), and the Pali language, and in recent years Theravada monastic leaders, with the support of government, have sought to raise the standard of these studies. In Thailand the concern for up-grading Dhamma and Pali-language studies goes back to King Mongkut (Rama IV) in the nineteenth century. As a Bhikkhu Mongkut mastered the Pali texts and in 1833 founded an elite order of monks, the Dhammayuttikanikaya.

The Dhammayuttikanikaya distinguished itself from the larger body of Thai monks (Mahanikaya) by its concern for a thorough understanding of the Pali language and liter-ature and purity in keeping the monastic discipline. King Mongkut's son, Prince Vajiranana in 1893 founded an insti-tute for higher Dhamma and Pali studies at Wat Borvor-nives, the Mahamakuta Rajavidyalaya in Bangkok. Three years earlier (1890) King Chulalongkorn (Rama V) had founded a similar institute at Wat Mahadhatu, the Maha-dhatu Vidyalaya.[34] In 1910 as Supreme Patriarch (San-kharat) of the Thai order, Vajiranana instituted national standards for Dhamma and Pali studies which are still in force. According to these standards the monks are to study toward examinations and certificates in three levels of Dhamma studies — Third, Second, and First Class Nak Dhamma;[35] and seven levels of Pali studies, Third through Ninth Class Parien.[36] Completion of both courses takes from seven to ten years. In 1967 there were 6,634 Nak Dhamma schools throughout Thailand with 14,474 monk-teachers and 30,000 students[37] and 615 Pali schools with 1,964 monk-teachers and 10,000 monk-students.[38] The two *wat* institutes in Bangkok, now known as Mahamakuta Rajavidyalaya and Mahachulalongkorn Rajavidyalaya, were raised to the status of universities in 1945 and 1947, respectively. In addi-tion to basic Dhamma and Pali instruction they now offer a Bachelor of Arts degree in Buddhist studies. Their programs will be discussed below.

Burmese monks have always prided themselves on their Dhamma and Pali scholarship; every monastery (*kyaung*) is a school (*kyaung*), for the monks as well as the laity. Prior to British rule it was the duty of the king to set Pali exami-nations for the monks and duly honor those who passed.

The British government continued administration of these examinations and each year increasing numbers of monks stood for them.[39] In 1950, under the Pali University and Dhammacariya Act, the Burmese government began to upgrade Dhamma and Pali studies creating a system of *kyaungs* recognized as "colleges" under a Central Council of the Pali University. Kyaungs qualified as colleges by having at least ten monk-scholars who had passed the Patamagyi ("higher standard") Pali examination. In 1962 eighty-four *kyaungs* were affiliated with the Pali University Council, each having a representative on the council. The Pali Education Board Act of 1952 placed the administration of all Pali examinations under a single board; the board is particularly concerned with the lower-level Pali examinations of which there are three grades (lower, middle, and senior). As with the Nak Dhamma in Thailand, laymen as well as monks may stand for the Pali examinations; in 1959; 12,433 persons took examinations in the three lower levels.[40]

Monastic education in Laos and Cambodia has been developed in a structure parallel to that of public education. Of the two systems, the Cambodian is the more efficiently organized and offers the higher quality instruction. In fact, the education available to the Cambodian monk is equal in quality and breadth to that available in Thailand and very much broader than that available in Burma.

There are approximately ninety-five Pali schools in Laos: ninety elementary, four secondary (at Vientiane, Thakhet, Savannakhet, and Pakse), and one Pali high school at Vientiane. These schools are administered by the Buddhist Institute in Vientiane which in turn functions under the Ministry of Religious Affairs. While the curriculum concentrates on the traditional subjects, Dhamma and Pali, at the secondary and high school levels it offers a number of courses in "secular" subjects, and it is hoped that sooner or later the Institute itself may become a university offering a liberal arts degree.

The Cambodian system includes approximately six hundred primary schools, two high schools (one in Phnom

Penh and one in Battambang), and the Preah Sihanouk Raj Buddhist University of Phnom Penh. The Preah Suramarit Buddhist High School in Phnom Penh, founded in 1955, offers a four-year program and admits 180 students each year. The University, founded in 1954, admits 40 students per year and now offers three courses of study leading to the doctorate in Buddhist studies.

The most impressive and significant development in monastic education in Theravada Southeast Asia has taken place not simply with the institution of "higher" education for the monks but with the introduction of a broad spectrum of "secular" subjects into the curriculum. The Vientiane High School and the universities in Phnom Penh and Bangkok are expressly concerned to educate the monk to a more effective exercise of his social role.

> The aim of the general course of studies given in the Pali High School [Vientiane] is to give the elite of the Sangha a sense of their responsibilities when faced with the dangers threatening the nation in which they play a very important part.[41]

Among the aims of the Preah Sihanouk Raj Buddhist University is the following, which speaks of the concern of Buddhist educators in Thailand and Laos as well:

> To enable Cambodian Buddhist monks to know all branches of knowledge including both aspects of life: the Buddhist aspect as well as the modern aspect for a suitable living in a society, as we know very well all the countries all over the world in this age are marching towards the enlightened step of education. Moreover, Buddhist monks in Cambodia are the backbone of the public in the field of directing it to a prosperous goal. If monks are kept illiterate, we feel that the public is surely bound to suffer the same ailment which must be cured by first educating monks.[42]

The course of studies in the university includes courses in psychology, sociology, history (Cambodian and world), mathematics, physics, English, French, Hindi, Chinese, political economics, hygiene, and so forth.

The Thai Buddhist universities offer a similar liberal arts curriculum and, in addition, some very practically oriented subjects. Mahamakut University offers courses in Electric Equipments Used in Daily Life, Health Education, and Social Institutions and Social Changes. Mahachulalongkorn has three faculties — Buddhist Studies, Education, and Humanities and Social Welfare. The Humanities and Social Welfare faculty has as its purpose:

> to cover the Humanities and those branches of the Social Sciences that will help the monks in their effective relationship with the people and in their observing their duties toward society *especially in community development*.[43]

The curriculum includes courses offered by laymen as well as monks on such subjects as: Community Development in Thailand, The Thai Minorities, Cultural Anthropology, Public Administration, Economics and Social Development, and Education in Thailand. Mahachulalongkorn's Teacher Training College aims ". . . to produce monastic teachers at the elementary level in response to the need of the nation for qualified teachers in provincial schools both monastic and secular."[44] The admissions policy gives special consideration to monks from the up-country who will return to teach and aid social development in their province. Beyond the degree curriculums offered by these universities both schools have in the past six years introduced special short-term study programs — Mahamakut training monks for hill-tribe missions and foreign missions, and Mahachulalongkorn training up-country monks in social service.

Burmese Buddhists have not moved effectively to provide a higher, liberal arts education for the monk.[45]

The education of the monk is a critical issue for those concerned with the survival of the Buddhist way in the face of rapid change. Not all Buddhists are happy with the trends in higher education for the monk. Opponents, mostly laymen, argue that a liberalizing education is secularizing, tending the Bhikkhu away from his traditional learning and role and away from the purity of life which commands the respect of the society. Further, they argue, a significant number of men of high potential have left the Sangha after receiving a higher education. It is somewhat commonly said in Laos, "When they learn English, they leave the order and go to work for the U.S.I.S. (United States Information Service)." Supporters of a broader education for the monk retort that if the monk is to continue to be a strong influence in maintaining the Buddhist way of life, he must be at least as broadly educated as the laity he serves. The Bhikkhu who is ignorant of the ways of a "modernizing" world will be bypassed or perhaps wrongly used by forces antithetical to Buddhism and the welfare of the nation.

The Organization of the Sangha

In accordance with the reported last words of the Buddha, the Dhamma is to be the monk's sole guide. Every monk has direct access to the Dhamma. Further, the rules and regulations of the monastic life as given in the Pali Canon are considered final and cannot be altered. Thus, authority in the Sangha is strictly administrative according to seniority and official appointment. The new initiate to the monastic life must sit at the feet of the elder monks, and even among the elders, seniority according to years as a Bhikkhu must be recognized. It is to be assumed that greater years as a monk brings greater wisdom and self-discipline. After ten years as a Bhikkhu a monk is considered a Thera ("elder") and after twenty years as a Bhikkhu he is considered a Mahathera ("great elder").[46] Seniority of years in the order is recognized whenever monks are together, chanting in private, or being publicly honored, and only those of Thera rank and above are qualified to ordain.

As the early followers of the Buddha began to take up a settled life in monasteries it became necessary for them to formulate regulations ordering the life of Bhikkhus and novices living together in one place. These regulations are embodied in the Pali Canon, particularly the Patimokkha of the Vinaya texts,[47] and are therefore as binding on Theravada monks as the Buddha-word itself, and cannot be altered.

As the Sangha grew in numbers and strength under official patronage in Ceylon and Southeast Asia, monastic and government leaders moved to regulate the life of the monk on a national basis making for greater efficiency of Sangha administration and greater government control. In Thailand, Laos, and Cambodia where Buddhism is officially established, Sangha administration is organized on the same basic pattern as government. Each *wat* is administered by an abbot who may be assisted by other monks and laymen depending on the number of monks under his care.

In Thailand the *wat* is identified in a subdistrict, district, province, region, and area. Each of these divisions has a chief monk in charge of his division and responsible to the chief of the next higher jurisdiction. The national Sangha is administered overall by a council of elder Bhikkhus — the Supreme Sangha Council under a supreme patriarch, the Sangharaja. The Sangharaja is appointed by the king on the recommendation of the Supreme Sangha Council. Members of the council are appointed by the king and the Sangharaja from among those monks recognized as Mahatheras. The chief monks of each division of the Sangha are selected by the chiefs of the next lower division in concurrence with the chief of the next superior division and the equivalent civil authorities; e.g., the chief of a subdistrict is selected by the abbots of the *wats* within that subdistrict subject to the approval of the district chief and government officials at district and subdistrict levels. Every monk is registered and required to carry papers indicating where, when, and under whom he was ordained. In matters of monastic rules and regulations, the individual may be urged on or reprimanded by his abbot and fellow monks but he is responsible only to himself, except in the case of major offenses. In the event of a monk committing an act of theft, murder, sexual misconduct, vainglory,[48] or any act considered criminal by civil law, the offender is tried by a group of his superiors and if found guilty defrocked and, if appropriate, turned over to civil authorities.

Formal relationships between the government and the Sangha are carried on through the king and the Department of Religious Affairs in the Ministry of Education. The director-general of the Department of Religious Affairs, a layman, is secretary to the Supreme Sangha Council. In addition to participating in this way in the proceedings of the Supreme Sangha Council, the Department of Religious Affairs collaborates with the Supreme Sangha Council on various Sangha programs, oversees monastic education, keeps vital statistics on monks and *wats* supplied by abbots and divisional chiefs, oversees the maintenance of *wat* buildings and grounds, and initiates programs of its own relative to lay education and youth work. The Thai government recognizes and patronizes all religions practiced in the kingdom and therefore, the Department of Religious Affairs is also the channel of government patronage to the non-Buddhist groups.

Sangha administrative order in Laos and Cambodia is basically the same as that of the Thai Sangha. The Lao Sangha is ordered in terms of fewer divisions: *wat*, subdistrict, district, and province, council of elders, and Sangharaja. The Cambodian Sangha is ordered in terms of *wats*, districts, and provinces, is under a chief of state rather than king, and has no national council of elders. The chief monks of the Cambodian Sangha meet in Phnom Penh once a year and thereby exercise somewhat the same authority and leadership that are exercised by the councils of elders in Thailand and Laos. Both the Lao and the Cambodian Sanghas are related to government through a Ministry of Religious Affairs.

At the time of the British take-over in Burma, the Burmese Sangha, under royal patronage, was organized much as the Thai Sangha is today. The monks apparently recognized several patriarchs (Thathanabaing or Sangharaja), but the king honored only one as supreme.[49] This structure, for the most part, lapsed during the British period. Today the monks are organized in autonomous *kyaungs* or monasteries each under an abbot. In the larger centers of population, clusters of *kyaungs* are ordered as *kyaungtaiks* under a single head. There are a number of regional chief monks but they apparently have title without power.[50] Beyond the *kyaungtaiks* many of the monks are organized in associations, the most significant of which are the All Burma Young Monks Association (Yahanpyu Aphwe), founded in 1938, and the All Burma Presiding Monks Association, founded in 1955 and open only to senior monks (*sayadaws*). According to its general secretary, the Young Monks Association had 21,000 members in 1963.[51] Although Buddhism was not officially established, in 1950 the government of Burma formed a Ministry of Religious Affairs. This ministry dispenses funds toward the advancement of Buddhism and has stimulated the formation of a number of lay and monastic, nongovernmental organizations such as the Union Buddha Sasana Council (lay) and the All Burma Presiding Monks Association. None of these instruments has been able to effect overall control of the Sangha, even to the point of registering the monks.[52] Under the Vinasaya Act of 1949 a system of courts was established whereby cases involving monks and monastic property would be tried by a panel of *sayadaw* judges under monastic law. Throughout the 1950s there were complaints from the monks, particularly those *sayadaws* who sat on the courts, that some of the courts were not functioning properly and many of them were not functioning at all.[53] In 1961, by the passage of the Constitution (Third Amendment) Bill and the State Religion Promotion Bill, Buddhism became the established religion of Burma. The provisions of these bills would have placed Burmese Buddhism on much the same footing as Buddhism in Thailand or Cambodia but most of these provisions never came into effect and those that did were repealed shortly after the Ne Win government took charge in 1962. The Union Buddha Sasana Council was abolished in 1962 and the Vinasaya Act of 1949, the Pali University and Dhammacariya Act of 1950, and the Pali Education Board Act of 1952 were repealed in 1965.[54] Presumably, the Ministry of Religious Affairs is still functioning but on a very small budget and with practically no instrumentalities by which to patronize Buddhism.

It appears that the present government of Burma has decided not to officially foster Buddhism:

> A representative of the Revolutionary Council declared that its policy was one of "minimum participation by the government in religious affairs" . . .[55]

It is quite clear, however, that the governments of Thailand, Laos, and Cambodia desire close working relationships with the Sangha and desire to foster Buddhism among the people. It is evident that all of these governments recognize the actual and potential power of the monks over the mass of the people and therefore seek to control and channel the exercise of this power. A unified and reasonably content, i.e., well-patronized Sangha is a critical force for stability in the nation as is clearly the case in Thailand and Cambodia. On the other hand, a fragmented, malcontent Sangha is a factor making for instability in the nation as is clearly the case in Burma and Laos. Tradition dictates that it is the province of government to ensure unity and prosperity in the Sangha.

The Thai government seems to be most affirmatively supportive and effectively in control of the Sangha. There are two major avenues of government patronage of the Sangha. One is the operation of the Department of Religious Affairs — the budget of the Department of Religious Affairs for 1965 was 14,000,000 baht, four million of which was expanded in subsidy payments to high-ranking monks and eight million of which was expended for temple repairs. The other avenue of government Sangha-support, and perhaps the more important in the eyes of the people, is royal and official merit-making. Many of the elaborate, originally Brahmanical rituals once performed at the Thai court legitimizing the king and promoting the general welfare of the nation have been simplified or altogether discontinued. But the key Buddhist rituals in which the king leads the nation in making merit by honoring the Buddha and the monk on such occasions as Vesakha[56] and Kathin[57] are very much in evidence, publicized throughout the country. Thai government and Sangha leaders desirous of promoting order and unity in the Sangha (and thereby, order and unity in the society), safeguarding Sangha self-rule, and maintaining firm government control of the Sangha have taken care to redefine the working relationship of Sangha and government in the light of change. The following from the foreword of a 1963 publication on the government acts concerning administration of the Sangha sums up the ideal very well:

> This . . . is not an imposition of the Government's will on the community of Sangha, which has already the Patimokkha or the Code of Discipline for the Order as the guide and framework of its behaviour. Rather it is due to the changing circumstances following the complexities of living in the modern world. This necessitates a close cooperation and mutual understanding between the State and the Sangha working harmoniously together for the economic and the spiritual well-being of the people. Such an Act, based always on the advice and consent on the part of the Sangha, also serves to maintain the solidarity of the Bhikkhu community as a whole, resulting in the fact that the Buddhist Order of Thailand is systematically organized and knows where it stands in the whirl and the pressure of modern life.[58]

Maintaining Sangha self-rule and government control requires fine balancing — perhaps too fine to be actual. The Act on the Buddhist Brotherhood of 1941 essentially decentralized Sangha administration in line with the constitutional monarchy instituted in 1932. The 1962 Act on the Administration of the Buddhist Order of Sangha revised Sangha structure in order to return control to the center. These Sangha-administration acts indicate the duties and privileges of the Sangha council and the various Sangha officials, provide that all monks and monasteries be registered with the Department of Religious Affairs, establish penalties for monks who refuse to respect the ruling of their superiors concerning their conduct, and declare the Department of Religious Affairs to have oversight of all Sangha activities. Leading monks consistently emphasize that Sangha and government are the two wheels of the cart which is the nation and in order for the nation to prosper the 'wheels' must move together. Given this two-wheel theory, it is conceivable that the Sangha could be antigovernment, passive, or progovernment. The Thai have never known any significant antigovernment activities within the Sangha and at present the majority of monastic leaders are tacitly progovernment. In fact, to these leaders it is inconceivable that Thai monks would engage in antigovernment activities such as have the monks of Burma, Ceylon, and South Vietnam.

The relationship between Sangha and government in Laos and Cambodia is formally defined in much the same terms as it is in Thailand, and royal and official patronage of the Sangha is clearly in evidence, especially in Cambodia. As the French did not interfere with the structure of the Sangha or its relationship to monarchy in these kingdoms, the tie with ancient tradition remains unbroken as in Thailand. Former Chief of State Sihanouk, although having given up the throne, had taken great pains to identify with the Khmer tradition concerning kingship and the Sangha. While taking care that the autonomy of the Sangha and its individual leaders were properly recognized and respected, he had promoted such a close working relationship between government and Sangha that the monks were practically government agents. By the fact of his lineage and his personal charisma, Sihanouk enjoyed a very special relationship to the Cambodian Sangha; and, no doubt, his absence has occasioned some change in Sangha-government relationships. However, this author has no reason to believe that the recent coup has altered these relationships in any fundamental way.

The Lao Sangha does not enjoy the unity evident in the Thai and Cambodian Sanghas, and the royal government does not enjoy the degree of control over the Sangha which the Thai and Cambodian governments exercise. From time to time the Pathet Lao as well as the royal government have made various overtures for support from the monks and of course monks residing in Pathet Lao controlled areas are not effectively controlled by the royal government. Loyalties among the monks are as divided as those of the Lao people generally, and the Sangha does not at present appear to be a strong force for unity and stability in the country.[59]

At the point when the Thai were moving to unify the Sangha administratively and formalize its relationship to government, the British in Burma were permitting what order and unity existed in the Burmese Sangha to lapse. The Burmese Sangha lacked strong unifying leadership throughout the British period. It suffered apparently irreversible fragmentation due to the overt anti-British political activities of a significant number of leading *pongyis*. Unlike independent Laos and Cambodia, established as Buddhist nations, Burma was initially established as a 'secular' state. Even though the U Nu government honored and extensively patronized the Sangha and Buddhism generally, sponsored a national and international council of monks, and finally established Buddhism as the State Religion, it not only failed to promote effective order and unity in the Sangha, but also, at one and the same time, aggravated non-Buddhist minorities of the country and prominent Buddhists of the majority who saw government patronage of Buddhism as an unjustifiable drain on the national economy. Ne Win and Buddhist members of his government have not publicly disavowed their Buddhism,[60] yet they have made it clear that government has no intention of promoting Buddhism, and antigovernment *pongyi* political activity will not be tolerated. Even so, in 1965 immediately following the arrest of ninety-two politically active monks on charges of corruption Ne Win dispatched soldiers throughout the country to clean up monastery grounds and buildings.[61] The following 1958 statement by U Kyaw Thet would still seem in order:

> Today, the phongyis' training is still almost entirely religious, not secular, but there is no question that the Sangha indirectly influences some government decisions. To be sure, the Order is not organized on a national basis; there is no primate directing a hierarchy — its structure is decentralized. But undoubtedly there is consultation between officials and the monks at many levels, and it would be a foolhardy politician who took a position or attempted to push through a program that was clearly displeasing to the clergy. . . . It is clear, then, that the planners who are building a new Burma must reckon with the Sangha in all their thinking.[62]

All of the Theravada Sanghas of Southeast Asia have experienced a reform movement such that there are presently two distinct groupings of monks within each national Sangha. In Thailand, Laos, and Cambodia these two groups are known as the Mahanikaya or "Great Order" and the Dhammayuttikanikaya or the "Order of Those (Properly) Committed to the Dhamma." In Burma these groups are the Sudhamma or "Good Dhamma" Order and the Shwegyin.[63] The latter derives its name from the village of its founder. The monks of all these groups adhere to the same doctrine and discipline — that which distinguishes one group from another is basically the strictness of adherence to certain monastic regulations. The Mahanikaya and the Sudhamma are the older, less strict, majority groups. The Dhammayuttikanikaya and Shwegyin are reform groups founded in the nineteenth century. The former, founded in Thailand in 1833, was instituted in southern Laos about 1850 and in Cambodia in 1864 by monks trained in Thailand. The latter was founded in the reign of Mindon Min (1852–77).[64] Both groups are concerned with stricter adherence to the monastic discipline prescribed in the Pali Canon and greater emphasis on study and meditation. Thus, for instance, the monks of these orders will carry their alms-bowl in their hand rather than on a sling, will receive all kinds of food in the same container, will eat only once per day, and will more strictly keep the prohibitions on handling money and participating in any kind of entertainment. The Dhammayuttika monks of Thailand tend to spend more time in study and meditation and less in social affairs such as home rituals and community welfare programs than the Mahanikaya monks. This difference of emphasis is reflected in the recent programming of the two Thai Bhikkhu universities: Mahamakut, the Dhammayuttika school, taking up missionary programs; and Mahachulalongkorn, the Mahanikaya school, focusing on the role of the monk in social service.

Only a small minority of the monks belong to the reform orders, but those who join tend to remain monks for a longer time than those joining the older, less strict majority groups, and their influence on Sangha affairs has been considerable. In Thailand and Laos the Mahanikaya and Dhammayuttika groups are under the same hierarchy. In Burma and Cambodia the reform group has its own administrative structure. Laymen honor and serve all monks without distinction.

VI

The Monk and Society

> Go ye now, O Bhikkhus, and wander, for the gain
> of the many, for the welfare of the many, out of
> compassion for the world, for the good, for the
> gain, and for the welfare of gods and men. Let not
> two of you go the same way. Preach, O Bhikkhus,
> the doctrine which is glorious in the beginning,
> glorious in the middle, glorious at the end. . . .[1]

SOME WRITERS on Theravada Buddhism refer to the monks
as 'priests'. The use of such a term involves the Westerner
in the same difficulties of illegitimate transference as does
the use of the word 'monk'. The Bhikkhu in Buddhism
should not be seen as fulfilling the same role as the priest in
Western Catholicism. And yet, he is not simply a monk
quietly engaged in study and meditation within the monastery. In as far as the word 'priest' conveys the sense of
'mediator' or 'go-between', or even 'one who sanctifies', there
is a profound sense in which the Bhikkhu is a priest. In
many contexts the Bhikkhu passively radiates, mediates, the
Buddha-power to the lay society in which he lives.

The life of the novice is largely one of study, meditation, and giving assistance to the Bhikkhu. The Bhikkhu also

engages in study and meditation, but his status in the eyes
of the laity is greater than that of the novice, and he may
spend much of his time preaching, teaching, counseling,
healing, and even administering community projects. The
lay society exerts a general pressure upon the novice and
Bhikkhu to maintain at least a minimum standard of adherence to the monastic discipline and to properly officiate
in daily and special rituals. Beyond this, the degree of rigor
with which the monk undertakes study and meditation and
the extent to which the Bhikkhu performs in various social
service roles depend upon the will of the monk himself and
the attitude of his spiritual guide and abbot. Generally
speaking a monk of the Shwegyin or Dhammayuttika Orders
will be under greater pressure to study and meditate than
will a monk of the Sudhamma or Mahanikaya Orders.

All novices and Bhikkhus are committed to daily, morning, and evening meditation — chanting before the Buddha-
image. On these occasions the monks offer candlelight, incense, and flowers before the Buddha-image and under the
leadership of the abbot or other elder Bhikkhu intone the
threefold refuge and chant several Suttas from the Pali texts.
Hereby, they are reflecting on the Buddha-life and word
with Buddhahood imaged before them that they may
quicken their own self-discipline and understanding moving
along the path the Buddha blazed.

> While lighting the candle or lamp one reflects: "Oh
> may I become Perfectly Enlightened so that I am able
> to help enlighten others." From that flame, the incense
> sticks are lighted with the thought, "In order to achieve
> Perfect Enlightenment may the fragrance of my moral
> conduct spread among all beings, as this sweet incense
> is smelt in all directions." Then flowers are offered be-
> tween folded hands, thinking: "But this life is short and
> even though these flowers are fresh and beautiful to-
> day, tomorrow they will be faded and evil-smelling, —
> so it is with what I call my body."[2]

The Monk and Society

The threefold refuge recited by laymen as well as the monks
on almost every ritual occasion is a thanksgiving to the Buddhas of the past, present, and future and a reminding affirmation of the context in which one has chosen to live his
life:[3]

Namo tassa Bhagavato, Arahato, Sammasambuddhassa
Praise to the Blessed One, the Noble One, the
    Perfectly Enlightened One!

Buddham saranam gacchami
I go to the Buddha for refuge.

Dhammam saranam gacchami
I go to the Dhamma for refuge.

Sangham saranam gacchami
I go to the Sangha for refuge.[4]

Four times each lunar month — on the new moon, the
eighth day of waxing, the full moon, and the eighth day of
waning — the monks engage in a special ritual, the *Uposatha*. The Uposatha provides an occasion for the laity to come
to the monastery, meditate while listening to the chanting
of the monks, receive the precepts ("I undertake not to kill,"
etc.), and hear an elder Bhikkhu sermonize on the Buddha-
life and word and the merit accrued to those who participate
in the moon-day ceremony. This ritual is one of the most
ancient by which the monk dispenses merit to the laity.
Aside from major festivals, it is the only regularly occurring
ritual involving laymen as well as the monks. The layman
himself chooses to attend the Uposatha ceremony and must
request receipt of the precepts, but it is properly the monk
who administers the vows and delivers a sermon and there
is special meaning in these occasions simply by the presence
of the monks. Thus, while strictly speaking the monk is not
required for the precepts ritual, he has in fact become the
minister of the occasion. On the days of the new-moon and
full-moon Uposatha, the Bhikkhus recite the Patimokkha of

the Vinaya texts, after which, in pairs according to seniority, they exhort each other to keep the discipline of the monastic life.[5]

The monks have daily contact with the laity in receiving food. Early each morning, carrying his alms-bowl, the Bhikkhu makes himself available before the houses of the laity to receive food offerings. We may say that he is begging. Actually, he is providing opportunity to the layman to earn merit through giving. The Bhikkhu is indifferent — he should not care whether he eats or what he eats. While he receives and eats this food he is to think, 'I eat in order to sustain my body, not in order to enjoy eating'. Of course, we recognize, as do the Bhikkhu and layman themselves, that the Bhikkhu must eat to live and that if he is to eat, food must be provided by the layman since the monastic discipline prohibits the Bhikkhu from raising and cooking his own food. But this is to miss the beauty and profound meaning of a simple, necessary act, sacralized. The staff of life is given and received in recognition and cultivation of the spirit of 'giving up' or sacrificing on the part of layman and humbly receiving on the part of the Bhikkhu. The power of the Buddha-life and word is mediated.

Patterns of food-gathering vary from one country to another and one village to another. In Thailand the Bhikkhus go out in all directions alone or accompanied only by a temple boy or novice to help carry the food. In Laos, the Bhikkhus go out in a long line and together pass along the same route. The Bhikkhu may not always eat the food he receives; laywomen often provide the meal at the appropriate time at the monastery itself and the food collected by the Bhikkhu is given to animals wandering the monastery compound. Moerman reports that in Ban Ping groups of households take turns in providing food at the monastery, and the monks do not make the ritual round.[6]

Uposatha preaching and teaching and receipt of food are the two most frequent regular occasions on which the Bhikkhu dispenses merit to the society. On numerous other occasions such as a marriage, opening a new home, the birth of a child, birthdays and deaths, and public dedications the Bhikkhus are invited into the home or to a public gathering to 'bless' the occasion by their presence and especially by chanting the Buddha-word and showering those present with 'holy' water. For example, in Thailand, an odd number of monks are invited for auspicious occasions (birthday), an even number for inauspicious ones (funeral). For a birthday or housewarming the monks seat themselves on the floor in a line and in order of seniority (the number of Vassa or Rain Retreats one has been a monk) and grasping a string tied at one end to the Buddha-image of the domestic shrine, then around the base of a water vessel, and fixed all around the house and yard, chant appropriate selections from the Pali Canon. The power of the Buddha-word and the purity of the monk are carried through the string, making it a 'hot line' such that everything it touches and every person and thing within the area marked off by the string is 'blessed'.[7] In chanting the monks hold a large fan in front of their faces in order that their concentration and purity of thought may not be disturbed by looking upon the person or activity of others present (particularly women). For elder monks the fan may have great meaning as its insigne indicates his status and the fan itself may have been presented by the king or other high dignitary. Following the chanting, the laity present gifts to the monks, such things as they can use (toilet tissue, razor blades, etc.), the head Bhikkhu showers the laity with water from the string-encircled vessel, and a member of the household pours water as a means of conveying (sharing) the merit of the occasion with all beings, especially recently deceased members of the family. If the ceremony is held in the morning hours, the monks are then offered food. Through such rituals the lay and monastic lives are constantly kept in context.

The Bhikkhu most actively influences the life-style of the lay society in his role as teacher. As the learned master of the Buddhist way one of his primary responsibilities is to educate the temple boys and novices under his care in the basic tenets of Buddhism. In the precolonial period the monastery was the sole center of learning, and the Bhikkhus taught village boys reading and writing the vernacular language and manual arts, as well as the fundamentals of Buddhism. The Christian mission schools trained Buddhists as well as Christians but even at the height of mission activity they touched a very small portion of the Buddhist population. The British in Burma and the French in Laos and Cambodia encouraged 'secular', Western-oriented education and managed to 'modernize' the curriculum of a few monastery schools but without great effect on the mass of the population in the villages. With the coming of independence, elementary education in Burma, Laos, and Cambodia was still largely in the hands of the monks following the traditional curriculum. The government of Thailand began to develop a public school system in the late nineteenth century[8] and in 1921 established minimum standards for elementary education requiring girls as well as boys to attend school to fifteen years of age or through the fourth level. Following independence the governments of Burma, Laos, and Cambodia moved in a like manner. All of these governments encouraged the monastery schools to broaden their curriculum, train girls as well as boys, and thereby become part of the national educational system. If not by preference this encouragement came out of necessity as government was unable to provide enough buildings and lay teachers to meet the need.

The development of government schools without reference to the monk and monastery has somewhat affected the role of the Bhikkhu in education not so much by excluding him from teaching (as some suggest) as by creating a new kind of educator. To an extent, and mostly in the cities and larger towns, the Bhikkhu as teacher of reading and writing has been displaced by lay educators. Yet the great majority of the monastery schools are still functioning, some within the government system and some on purely traditional lines, and, even in the larger centers of population, the Bhikkhu continues in his role as teacher of the Buddhist way. The government school system has not so much replaced monastery schooling as it has made it possible for more young people to receive a primary education. In general terms the monk as educator is now rivaled by the lay teacher, but he is still master of the teaching of Buddhism and to a significant extent participates in the 'modern' school system.

In Thailand almost half of the primary schools are *wat* schools taught by monks as well as laymen. Only 20 percent of the primary school students are studying in *wat* schools but the number of primary students taught by monks has actually increased since compulsory education was introduced. In 1965 the number of new *wat* schools built was 1,605 and, as we have noted, government and Sangha leaders are presently encouraging monks to train for teaching not only in *wat* schools but also in non-*wat* schools. The Cambodian government has encouraged monk-teachers and *wat* schools as strongly as the Thai government. In 1967 one-half of the primary schools were *wat* schools taught almost exclusively by monks. These schools serviced 10 percent of the primary school children. In Laos in 1959 approximately 23 percent of schools were *wat* schools (334 out of 1,481) and 10 percent of primary school students were taught by monks in these schools. This represented an increase of 106 schools and 2,100 students over 1957.[9] In Burma neither the government nor the monks themselves have taken significant steps toward bringing the monk and the monastery school into the mainstream of modern education. The British encouraged *pongyi-kyaungs* to broaden their curriculum and become part of a national primary school system but very few of these schools responded positively. In 1952, 73 percent of the schools providing education to primary age children on government standards were *pongyi-kyaungs* and 27 percent of the children in school were serviced by these monastery schools. Even so, the curriculum of most of the monastery schools has changed little from the traditional — the *pongyis* have had a very limited opportunity to receive training for teaching 'secular' subjects. The State Religion Promotion Act of 1961 made religious education in the schools compulsory and affirmed that in the further development of the primary educational system preference should be given to upgrading existing monastery schools or founding new schools within the monasteries. The Ne Win government has not honored this act and has given no encouragement to the monastery schools. Yet, the *pongyi* and *kyaung* are far from phased out of education. As long as there is no viable alternative, the great mass of the Burmese people living in rural areas will continue to rely on the *pongyi-kyaung*.

> Although the number of government schools is growing from year to year, the number of Burmese children who receive their first education at a monastery school is still in the majority.[10]

> There is no doubt but that a system of secularized education has lessened the influence of the monk among segments of the population who find no "market value" in a *pongyi kyaung* education, but in rural Burma the astonishing vitality of Buddhism must be attributed to the continuing religious education and the belief that an entirely secular education is only half an education.[11]

Depending on his personality, education, and special skills, and his 'success' in such matters, the Bhikkhu of some years in the Sangha may spend much of his time engaged in personal counseling. Having cultivated purity of living and the wisdom of the Buddha and thus being indifferent to worldly affairs (without an axe to grind) the Bhikkhu is sought out for counsel on marital problems, farming, business adventures, community concerns, the exorcism of malevolent spirit-beings. While the Pali scriptures prohibit the

Bhikkhu from engaging in such arts as astrology, sorcery, and divination and there are generally available nonmonks specialized in these arts, it is not unusual to find the abbot or other elder monk calculating auspicious and inauspicious times, places, and relationships, dispensing charms, and exorcising spirits by chanting Parittas or formulas taken from the Buddha-word. To many urban dwellers as well as villagers these ancient 'sciences' are very meaningful and who is a more appropriate practitioner than the learned, powerful Bhikkhu. Only the most sophisticated and somewhat Westernized Buddhist will complain about this practice. On occasion one can observe the learned Bhikkhu dealing with personal crises in a manner not unlike that of the modern psychiatrist but communicating in a language and a cosmological framework which the villager will understand and appreciate. Some few Bhikkhus have achieved regional and even national fame not unlike that of Western faith healers for their ability to charm away evil spirits. Dispensing medicines for physical ailments, concoctions of herbs, boiled tree roots, and the like, following a very ancient tradition is a quite common practice among the elder monks.

There is general agreement among those who have studied the way of the monk in Theravada Southeast Asia that the Bhikkhu has an important role as counselor on 'worldly affairs'. Pfanner found that his Burmese villagers preferred to take their personal problems to the headman rather than the monk,[12] but Slater reports the contrary:

> Perhaps the Order's most valuable service to the community is the function fulfilled by the monk as counsellor. A group of villagers may gather for a special instruction, others may attend when the monks assemble for devotions, but the monastery is not regarded as a preaching centre or as a place of public worship. In modern times, crowds have flocked to hear the Monyin Sayadaw. Generally, however, the approach in this respect is individual. It is as the individual adviser of

each villager that the monk's influence is most strongly felt.[13]

Worthy of special note in this matter is the extent to which Thai, Lao, and Khmer Bhikkhus counsel on problems of community development. In 1967 the author spoke with twenty to thirty Bhikkhus in various parts of Thailand, Laos, and Cambodia who were daily engaged in counseling on community welfare and development affairs and who considered this an important aspect of their responsibility to the lay society. Moerman, Ingersoll, Schecter, and Klausner, working in different parts of Thailand, support these findings. Ingersoll, reporting on villages in Central Thailand, cites activity which is fast becoming typical of Thai monks everywhere:

> People frequently talked with the headpriest about their farming difficulties, for which he had a deep concern. . . . Gradually and quietly the headpriest had become a strong village leader by expressing genuine concern for the well-being of the villagers, by undertaking energetic improvements in the temple which were of importance to the village as a whole, and by responding vigorously to the recent program of community development introduced by government officers. . . . At one cremation . . . . after the priests had finished reciting the chants . . . the headpriest gently began a quiet, earnest conversation with a circle of villagers to advocate moving ahead with the water improvement program![14]

Moerman's observation concerning Ban Ping in Northern Thailand gives a glimpse of the conflict of new and old attitudes and activities and the most frequently employed argument for change:

> When Ban Ping was unwilling to help construct a new school building, the district administrative officer came to the village with the district abbot. The abbot

118

preached a sermon in which he told the congregation that schools and roads make as much merit as temples because they bring about progress and call for cooperation.[15]

Merit-making as the way of lay Buddhism will be discussed in detail below. Klausner and Schecter make similar observations concerning Northeast Thailand, noting not only the monk's counseling but also his physical labor in community development. Klausner emphasizes the various ways in which the monks help meet basic social needs in an area where services normally provided by government are not available:

> The northeastern bhikkhus are generally very active in aiding the villagers to solve their everyday lay problems. In the northeastern villages, the bhikkhus and novices can be seen helping in the construction of a village well, the building of a bridge or small dam, the laying of a new village road, or the erection of a village meeting hall or school.[16]

The Bhikkhus give free medical aid, arbitrate personal quarrels, bank money at the *wat* for villagers, and even loan money from merit-contributions in time of emergency. Klausner appropriately explains the merit-interaction of monk and laity in very practical terms — the Bhikkhu has a know-how, a practical knowledge of use to the lay society, he is intimate with village life being in daily contact with it and having emotional ties to family, friends, and the village environment, and he has 'free time'; the layman meets the basic food, clothing, and shelter needs of the monk and expects something tangible in return.[17] Schecter records the comment of a monk urging community development in the face of official opposition:

> We Buddhist monks help the people spiritually but now we are starting to help them physically with community-development projects. Buddhist monks help

with wells and dams. I've even told the people not to worry about the police and to cut down logs for a dam. I showed them how to carry on the construction. The people respect the monks. Let them lead the development teams; then they will be successful.[18]

It is not adequately recognized that the monk as counselor on 'worldly' affairs and active agent in village social and economic affairs cannot but also be a political agent. Throughout Theravada Southeast Asia the laity rely on the elder Bhikkhu for counsel and aid on any and all matters of village life. Only overt antigovernment activity on the part of the monks such as has occurred often in Burma and on occasion in Laos and Cambodia[19] is noted as political. Many of the leading monks of Thailand and Cambodia are clearly progovernment and (especially in Thailand) anticommunist and in various subtle ways their words and activities make for political stability in their countries. Yet their influence is so subtle that neither the political analyst nor the monks themselves note it as political. Schecter's comment on Thai monks is applicable throughout the Theravada area:

> Everything monks do or say has a profound effect on the villagers. That inevitably includes a political effect if politics is defined as anything from organization of the village council to adoption of a village program.
>
> Thus, while Thailand's monks have seldom played an active political role in the sense that Buddhist monks have done in South Vietnam, their words and ways are so inextricably interwoven into the fabric of Thai village life that they have a profound political influence, whether they acknowledge or even want it.[20]

Whether or not the monk is viewed as a political agent seems to depend largely on the political persuasion of the viewer. Thus it is possible for an official of the Lao Ministry of Religious Affairs to comment:

The Monk and Society

It is possible for them [the monks] to be anti-communist and at the same time preserve our tradition of non-participation of the priesthood in politics. Thus, it is forbidden for the monks to work against the government, so they must support its program.[21]

And it is possible for Burmese Buddhists to celebrate the anti-British nationalistic activities of Burmese monks and decry *pongyi* political acts directed against the government of independent Burma. The issue of the monk in politics is not whether or not he should engage in political activity; rather it is what kind of political activity is appropriate to his status and role in particular circumstances and how supportive or oppositional is his activity to ruling power.

Community development and political activity on the part of the monk should not surprise us once we understand his status in the society and the way in which the monk and layman interact. We should expect to find the monk addressing himself to whatever problems are current among his people. In recent years Thai, Cambodian, and Lao monastic and government leaders have made a special effort to promote the effectiveness of the monk in these areas. Sangha and Department of Religious Affairs national programming in Thailand has been specifically geared toward education of the monk for effective leadership in village development and political integration. We have noted the Humanities and Social Welfare Curriculum of Mahachulalongkorn University. In 1966, in addition to regular offerings, Mahachulalongkorn instituted two short-term special study programs in community development and *wat* administration: a two-month course for university graduates who will reside in urban *wats*, and a six-month course for up-country monks, especially those who have not been through the university.[22] These programs stimulated the formation of several study centers throughout Thailand (Namkhai, Ubon, Udorn, and Chiengmai) offering social service seminars to local monks. Leadership of these special study programs is both lay and monastic, typically including the chief monks of the area, agricultural and educational experts, public health officials, and local government officials. The curriculum is geared to deal very practically with specific problems of public health, farming, construction, civil rights and duties, and the like. The following list of subjects from a Chiengmai seminar is representative:

1. Mental development (mental discipline)
2. People's rights and duties
3. Methods of approaching the community
4. Public health and hygiene (how to build a water-seal latrine)
5. Agricultural development
6. Food preparation and preservation
7. Village, *wat,* and school development
8. Methods of road and bridge building
9. Coordination and support from government offices and vocational support in the community
10. Physical training and recreation facilities

Most of the monks involved in these seminars are simply expected to return to their local community and put their new knowledge to work wherever and whenever possible in the normal course of affairs. Others will take part in a more systematic effort as members of development teams assigned to specific villages for a period of time. In 1968, twenty teams went out from Wat Phra Singh, headquarters of the Study Center and Development Mission in Chiengmai Province. These teams — including a monk-director, a monk Abhidhamma expert,[23] the chief monk of the district, district and subdivision officials, an agricultural expert, a medical doctor, and students from Chiengmai University — establish contact with local authorities (the abbot of the village *wat,* school teacher, headman), survey the particular needs of the village, and attempt to initiate programs to meet these needs. Each member of the team has his own job to do. The monk-director together with government officials will attempt to organize the villagers to undertake a particular task — bridge repair, building a school, road, or water pond, or rebuilding houses washed away in a recent flood. The Abhidhamma expert will preach and teach the Dhamma and perhaps try to set up a Nak Dhamma school. The team approach is conceived as an attempt at total uplift, speaking to both the physical and spiritual needs of the people. The social service seminars and the village missions are subsidized by grants from the Asia Foundation. Village development projects are largely financed by the villagers themselves, but on occasion rather large sums of 'seed' money are donated by the monks from the treasury of their *wat*.[24]

Mahamakut University has undertaken a similar program of training up-country monks for social service. In 1967 there were forty-three monks in training. The program has its sole base in the university in Bangkok, and is financed by the Asia Foundation and other private donors.[25]

One of the most interesting projects of the Thai Sangha is the Dhammajarig ("traveling Dhamma") Buddhist mission to the non-Buddhist hill tribes of Thailand initiated in 1963. This program is an excellent example of ideology and relationships basic to the Thai Buddhist way of life. The program was conceived by a former monk, now chief of the hill-tribes division of the Department of Public Welfare, and the abbot of one of the larger *wats* in Bangkok, Wat Benchama Borphit. It was approved by the Supreme Sangha Council, has its headquarters and training center at Wat Benchama Borphit, and has the financial and technical support of the Department of Religious Affairs and the Department of Public Welfare. The aim of the program is to bring Buddhism to the hill-tribes people. To do this is to assimilate the hill tribes into Thai culture; it is to socially, economically, and politically integrate them into the Thai national system.

In the third year of the program, 1966–67, one hundred monks (twenty teams of five) went into the tribal areas of Northern Thailand.[26] The monks are chosen by the chief monks of the northern provinces from a group of volunteers. Preference is given to those who speak a northern dialect, and who have a higher knowledge of the Dhamma or are graduates of one of the Bhikkhu universities. They receive one week of orientation at Wat Benchama Borphit in the customs and mores of the tribal people to whom they will be sent and in the aims and technique of their mission. The working period in the field is four months each year, March through June. The mission begins with passive presence. There is no attempt on the part of the monks to preach Buddhism or to degrade tribal religion. The Bhikkhus walk into the area (sometimes considerable distances) and quietly settle down explaining only that they have come for the welfare of the people. The Bhikkhus carry on the ritual of the monastic life, five being the minimum number of monks required for proper performance of the moon-day ceremonies (Uposatha or Wan Phra), their food being prepared and offered by temple boys who have accompanied them. If the villagers inquire as to the activities of the monks, the Bhikkhu takes the opportunity to begin to introduce Buddhist ideology. After some time, one to two months, the monks begin home-visits inquiring about the health and general welfare of each family. The information acquired is passed on to the Department of Public Welfare officials who may be in the immediate area or stationed at one of the several hill-operations bases established as part of a larger program. In 1967 there were twenty-nine teams of three government workers operating out of hill-operations bases, tribal research stations, and agricultural centers. If the home-visits are reasonably successful, the villagers begin to inquire more actively about the Buddhist way and gradually pick up the example of the temple boys in offering food and attending the ceremonies. The monk is counting on the villagers perceiving his way of life as exemplary — he does not drink or carouse; he is calm, sympathetic, and wise; he does not criticize the villager's way of life. Having established rapport, teaching elementary reading and writing and dispensing medicine (traditional practices of the Bhikkhu-way) are the basics of further development. In his teaching the monk necessarily introduces fundamentals of Thai culture — he tells the villagers of the king and queen and their concern for the welfare of the tribal peoples and tries to cultivate a positive attitude toward Thai government officials. Having observed the purity of the Bhikkhu's way of life, the villagers respect him and his teaching. The final state of the initial four-month mission is to encourage young men of the village to receive ordination into the Sangha. Some, especially the son or sons of the headman, are encouraged to train for government service. The ultimate success of the hill-tribes mission very much depends on this kind of active involvement of the tribal peoples in Thai culture. Continuing support of the Sangha will give the villager status in Thai society and the base for further education in the Thai Buddhist way. Governance in the Thai national system under members of their own ethnic group will assure loyalty.

It is as yet difficult to determine whether or not this program will have long-range success toward national unity. There is no doubt that the mission to the hill tribes is an attempt at political integration. At the present the program is being expanded into the Northeast, and the argument for its support appeals to anticommunist sentiment among monks and laity. Some influential monks and laymen are concerned that the Bhikkhus are being wrongly used by government. One layman even asserts that the Bhikkhus are being bribed to take part. However, Sangha and lay leaders who are involved in the project point out that it is a Sangha not a government program, that the monks freely participate, and the Vinaya or rules of monastic discipline are not violated.

Neither the Sangha nor government of Cambodia has organized special programs for training the monk in social service or political socialization. Yet, Cambodian monks are as active in these affairs as those of Thailand. Until recently the chief motivating and instructing force along these lines has been neither Sangha leadership nor the Buddhist university but former Chief of State Sihanouk. Sihanouk considered the Cambodian Sangha a key instrument of national integration and development, the heart of his Buddhist Socialist society.

> . . . our beloved Cambodia can progress only if there is simultaneous and harmonious progress from the point of view of the State and from the point of view of the Religion.[27]

He addressed groups of monks frequently and directed their activities by personal and government patronage. Since 1944 Sangha leaders have met annually in Phnom Penh to discuss Sangha affairs. For several years prior to the coup Sihanouk had been the keynote speaker praising the Bhikkhus for jobs well-done and apprising them of the state of the nation that they might be continually active in pacification and development. His remarks on the occasion of the Twenty-second Annual Congress in 1966 were typical:

> Our Buddhist Congress which is meeting today for the twenty-second time symbolizes the flowering and the radiance of our Buddhism not only in the sole domain of religion but also in those of the edification of our beloved people and the defense of our interests . . . our some 70,000 monks are the "officers" conducting our people to work, just as the officers conduct the troops into combat. . . . Many foreigners are ignorant of the true nature of Buddhism and the particular character of our Buddhism. They are astonished that such a leader as myself who aspires to obtain as rapid development as possible for my country would believe in Buddhism and attach such importance to it. They think of Buddhism as only a retrogressive philosophy, a handicap, an encouragement to the inertia and complacence of social stagnation.[28]

Sihanouk continued to say that foreigners did not understand Cambodian Buddhist Socialism. The aim of Buddhism in the age of the Sangkum[29] was not Nirvana, the perfection obtainable only after several thousands of reincarnations, but the alleviation of human suffering. Buddhist Socialism was not Marxist Socialism which seeks social justice by force. Buddhist Socialism was egalitarian and democratic, seeking social justice through national edification and state control and distribution of wealth. Foreign visitors were surprised at Cambodia's rapid development of education.

> This astonishingly rapid development is due in large part to the action of our clergy. . . . The Sangkum has, in effect, made of our Buddhism a dynamic religion which is becoming a powerful and effective auxiliary of the State for the task of national edification. . . .[30]

This was not pure rhetoric. Sihanouk maintained close contact with Sangha leaders seeking their advice and ensuring their favor toward his government. He donated sizable sums toward the uplift of the Sangha, most notable among these donations being a sum of 1,600,000 riels for the Secretariat and Library Building of Preah Sihanouk Raj Buddhist University.

The annual congress is also addressed by public health officers and educational and agricultural experts — in effect the congress of monks has become a national social service seminar. These meetings are duplicated at the district level. The monks have responded admirably. While it is difficult to document, my conversations with monastic leaders throughout the country indicate emphatically that the monks are the government's representatives among the people and contribute in large measure to law and order. They not only encourage community and national development but also engage in manual labor. School construction by monks is widespread. In 1966, the monks of ten *wats* in Siemreap joined forces to build a hospital. A major portion of the work on the railroad from Phnom Penh to Sihanoukville has been done by monks. For the past eight years, the Department of Health Services of the national government has been bringing small groups of monks to Phnom Penh for instruction in public health and basic first aid.

The kind of national Sangha development programming and activity well under way in Thailand and Cambodia is only beginning in Laos and is nonexistent in Burma. The level of social and political awareness and development programming in the Bhikkhu-Sangha depends upon the level and breadth of education of monastic and lay leaders and the financial resources available for development training. Significant numbers of Thai and Cambodian monks have had a higher education. Very few Lao and Burmese monks have had comparable training. There is some enthusiasm about development training for monks among the Lao Ministry of Religious Affairs and Sangha leaders, but there are apparently no funds available to support special programming. Inspired by the Thai social service seminars (in which some Lao monks took part) the monks of the Vientiane area, supported by the Asia Foundation, held a similar seminar in May of 1967. Approximately two hundred monks took part, the program was judged successful by those concerned, and seminars are being planned for the Luang Prabang and Pakse areas. Even so, there is as yet no basic commitment to this kind of effort on the part of Sangha national leaders and the Ministry of Religious Affairs.

The village *pongyi* in Burma enjoys the same high status as Bhikkhus elsewhere, and as in Thailand, Laos, and Cambodia, he serves his community as preacher, teacher, priest, counselor, and healer. Many urban *pongyis*, especially in the Rangoon and Mandalay areas, have been openly active in politics since the 1920s. Even so, there has been little inclination on the part of the monks, the government, or the laity generally toward 'modernizing' the Sangha and enhancing the role of the monk in social service and community development. The Buddhist revival of the 1950s emphasized Pali education, meditation, government patronage in the form of refurbishing old pagodas and building new ones, and official recognition of Buddhism as the State Religion.[31]

In his study of Buddhism and village economic behavior in Burma David Pfanner concluded:

> At the village level, the monk appears as neither an obstacle to nor promoter of economic development as far as his activities or attitudes are concerned.[32]

Political activity on the part of large numbers of urban monks appears to have fragmented rather than unified the Sangha. This activity together with a general indiscipline among the younger monks has adversely affected the monk's prestige in the eyes of the urban laity and apparently discouraged government from promoting a larger role for *pongyis* in national development.[33]

VII

The Way of the Laity

Whosoever, in this world gives gifts, and lives in righteousness, and keeps Uposatha, he, glad, . . . becomes filled with a sweet sense of trust and bliss ruling in his heart; his goodness grows still more and more abundantly. Like a deep pool of clear water, . . . and into which on one side the spring pours, while on the other the water flows away; so as it flows away it comes again, and there can be no failure there — so . . . does his goodness grow more and more abundantly.[1]

. . . he has practised so as to conquer both worlds; he tastes success both in this world and in the next.[2]

THE HIGH status and prominent role of the monk in the Theravada Buddhist way of life may make it appear that the layman is a Buddhist only as an auxiliary to the monk. Most textbooks on Theravada Buddhism leave the reader with this impression. In fact, the layman is as critically instrumental to the perpetuation of the Theravada way of life as is the monk. The monk exists to support the lay society as much as the layman exists to support the monk. The layman and the monk define each other's existence, exist for each other, and are catalysts to each other's way of life. By his purity and wisdom the monk moves the layman to acts of charity, respect, and reliance which in turn 'activate' the monk to compassionate service to society. That which characterizes the Theravada way of life is neither the way of the monk nor the way of the laity but the interaction, the reciprocation between the two. Ingersoll's comment on Thai Buddhism is applicable to the practice of Theravada Buddhism throughout Southeast Asia:

> The element of reciprocity is apparent here as it is in many Thai relationships. The priest acquires merit primarily through his monastic activities, made possible by the layman's complete material support, the supplying of which is the layman's chief means of acquiring merit. The priest in his parish activities too acquires merit by offering the layman opportunities for greater merit through temple and home rituals and by receiving the layman's merit-making material offerings in return. Whether priest or layman, the individual invariably acquires merit in exchange for some valued good, service, or sentiment offered to another person or persons.[3]

Even this allowance of equally important roles to layman and monk is an oversimplification. We must recognize two distinct categories of laymen in Theravada Southeast Asia. A significant number of adult males are former monks and as such they may enjoy a distinctly higher status and different role than the rest of the laity, providing a 'bridge' between monk and laity. It is the former monk who acts as lay ritual leader on such occasions as the Uposatha and in a number of rituals which do not require the leadership of the monk. Very often, and especially where a village has no long-term Bhikkhus in residence, the former monk performs functions normally performed by the monk himself.

The exemplar of this is Grandfather Iing, acknowledged by all to be "the most important person" in West Hamlet Kong. Age sixty-six, he had once been a monk for seven years and is now an achaa[4] much in demand for healing and for conducting private life-cycle and other ceremonies.[5]

There is a high correlation between having been a monk and holding formal or informal authority in village social and political affairs. This was notably the case in Ban Ping, Thailand:

> In Ban Ping, honor and even power are the rewards less of being a cleric than of having been one . . . . almost without exception the political leaders and moral counselors of the village have served in the temple . . . . almost all who have held the office of headman have been ordained. At village meetings, those who have been ordained monopolize the discussion. The informal village council is composed largely of the ordained. The committee that controls temple affairs has only one member who was never ordained. Litigants in trouble cases are likely to ask their ordained kinsmen to speak on their behalf. The lay leader of temple services and the aged authority on the spirits and the Buddha were both once priests.[6]

We have seen that the lay-life ideal has both personal and social dimensions and emphasizes 'giving', acts of charity. In sum, the layman is concerned with prosperity here and hereafter and to attain these goals he should keep the five precepts (refraining from killing, stealing, lying, sexual misconduct, and partaking of alcoholic beverages); he should honor and serve parents, teachers, husband, wife, children, friends, servants, and especially the monk; he should work hard, propitiate the spirits, amass wealth by honest means, live moderately, and give generously —

> The giving hand, the kindly speech, the life
> Of service, impartiality to one

As to another, as the case demands: —
These be the things that make the world go round
As linchpin serves the rolling of the car.[7]

These values are impressed upon the laity, male and female,
in manifold ways from birth onward. They are soaked up
osmotically by presence in an environment structured with
reference to monk and monastery. Every Buddhist has easy
access to monk and monastery — in fact, in most of the villages of Theravada Southeast Asia the monastery is the hub
of village life serving as school, social center, communica-
tions center, counseling and medical center, recreation area,
library, home for the aged and destitute, and social welfare
agency.[8]

Buddhist values are conveyed directly and indirectly
through formal education. The young males may study the
life and teachings of the Buddha as temple boys and/or
novices. Many of the larger *wats* of Thailand, Laos, and
Cambodia now offer Sunday school training to both girls
and boys. Lay and monastic leaders (especially in Burma
and Thailand) are presently concerned that religious education be part of the curriculum of all primary schools (government and monastic). The Thai Department of Religious
Affairs offers lay elementary school teachers a special course
in the teaching of Buddhism. Lay Buddhist organizations
such as the Young Men's Buddhist Association of Burma, the
Buddhist Association of Thailand, and the Young Buddhist's
Associations of Thailand and Laos aid in lay education by
sponsoring lectures on Buddhism and publishing and distributing pamphlets dealing with the life and teachings of
the Buddha and the principles of a householder's Buddhism.

Programs of formal education in Buddhism for the laity
are important to the continued vitality of the Buddhist way
of life, but Buddhist values are most widely and effectively
conveyed through daily, weekly, and occasional rituals performed in the home, in the field, at the village spirit-shrine
or in the monastery. In order to understand these rituals we

must first introduce the layman's concern with spirit-phe-
nomena.

The rituals of lay Buddhism are concerned with merit and
power, 'success both in this world and in the next' — merit
for a favorable rebirth and for status in society here and
now and power for the control of the spirit-forces which
condition worldly prosperity. As supporter of the Bhikkhu-
Sangha, the layman is necessarily concerned with prosperity
in worldly affairs; he understands the natural and social
environment in which he pursues worldly prosperity in
terms of spirit-forces — invisible beings whose activities
condition his physical and mental well-being. In order to
control these spirit-forces to the end of worldly prosperity
for the purpose of merit-making, he calls upon the power of
the Buddha and the monk and, consequently, his concern for
merit and his concern for power over spirits are inseparable
— i.e., he understands merit-making acts as a means to
power over the spirits which condition the prosperity he
needs in order to perform merit-making acts.[9]

The animistic beliefs and practices of the various Buddhist peoples of Southeast Asia differ in their outward form
but functionally they everywhere serve the same ends. Each
of the valued forces in the individual and his environment
has or is a spirit. The status and role of each spirit and its
relative importance in relation to other spirits are a reflection
of the particular social, economic, and political life of a
people (their history, way of livelihood, and social and political structures). There are nature-spirits — spirits of trees,
rocks, waters, mountains, rice paddy, and the like — spirits
of the dead, spirits of disease, and spirits of the household
and the land. The heavenly bodies are great spirits and their
movements affect human beings and their affairs. The spirits
which receive the most frequent and/or regular attention
are those relating to personal health, family life, and agriculture. The spirits most fearfully respected are those of the
dead. Men and other animals have spirits which continue to
exist after the death of the body and continue to influence

worldly affairs. These spirits tend to wander until they take on another body, and they may cause trouble if they are not cared for by embodied spirits during this period. The spirits of human beings who died violent or unusual deaths are particularly malicious, attacking newborn babies, causing serious illness, and the like and must be propitiated, placated, or frightened off by special means.

We may classify animistic belief and practice as superstition, but this only hinders us from understanding the function of spirit-veneration in the Buddhist way of life and from appreciating the 'animisms' in our own way of life. In a large sense, the animistic orientation to the world serves the same end as the scientific orientation; both seek to understand and manipulate man and his environment, both have specialists who work with hypotheses and theorems to develop 'laws' and who have devised special instruments of understanding and manipulation. The Buddhist sees the entire universe as alive, animated; so as to deal more directly and effectively with such a universe he personifies the various forces he perceives at work, collects data on their activities, and when needful employs this understanding in manipulating these forces to his own welfare (mental and physical well-being).

In Burma, the most important spirits are the 'Nats' — anything and everything which holds power may be designated 'Nat'. The Buddha, a king; forests, trees, waters, mountains, and fields, all have a guardian spirit or Nat. The most prominent Nats are the 'thirty-seven', thirty-six of which are held to be the spirits of particular human beings who met violent or unusual deaths. The thirty-seventh is Thagyamin, king of the Nats (Sakka, king of the Devas in canonical Buddhism).[10] In addition to Thagyamin, the most significant of the Nats are Eindwin-Min Mahagiri, "Lord of the Great Mountain who is also within the house,"[11] the Mizaing-Hpazaing Nats (particular Nats of the household inherited through the mother's (*mizaing*) and father's (*hpazaing*) family line), and the village and regional guardian spirits. Thagyamin is never localized; he keeps the records of merits and demerits and once a year — two days before the New Year — descends to the earth marking the beginning of the New Year festival. Min Mahagiri is the single most prominent Nat, being at one and the same time Lord of the Great Mountain, Guardian of the Nation, residing on Mount Popa, and Lord of the individual household honored by a coconut hanging within the house. According to Burmese folklore Min Mahagiri was a handsome blacksmith in the kingdom of Tagaung of such prowess that the king of the land felt threatened and tried to arrest him. Being unsuccessful in this, the king, having taken the blacksmith's sister as queen, lured the blacksmith ("Mr. Handsome") to capture saying that he was no longer a threat but a brother. Thereupon the king burned Mr. Handsome, the beautiful sister threw herself into the flames, and both became powerful spirits whose anger must be continually appeased by proper offerings.[12] In the course of time the Brother and Sister Nats were enshrined on Mount Popa as Lords of the Great Mountain and Min Mahagiri as Guardian of the Household. The coconut, hung in the southeast corner of the home, is offered to this Lord since its cold milk soothes his burns.[13]

There is a Nat-guardian for each level of sociopolitical involvement: household, larger family, village, region, and nation. Min Mahagiri is honored daily and on all special occasions. The Mizaing-Hpazaing Hereditary Nats, guardian spirits of the family line, are honored in family rituals, the child-naming, wedding, *shinbyu*, illness, and death. On occasions involving all or a large part of the village population — *shinbyus*, festivals, epidemic, change of location — the Village Nat must be honored.

The villagers say that the nat looks after the village as a grandfather looks after his family, i.e., he is concerned with their general welfare rather than, as a father would be, their daily maintenance. By his presence he guards

136

the village against strange nats and even human invaders, just as the house nat, like a sentry box, serves as a warning to anyone who wishes to do harm to members of the household.[14]

Some few Village Nats are so famous as to be honored throughout a region and the festivals to these Nats, such as that offered to the Taungbyon Brothers in Upper Burma, are major occasions for transvillage socializing. Under the U Nu government notable attention was paid the Nats as guardians of the nation. Donald Smith reports that:

> In 1951 sacrificial offerings were made to the nats at the prime minister's house by the members of his cabinet "to invoke the blessings of the spirits for the peace and prosperity of the country."[15]

In 1961 the U Nu cabinet voted to erect a new State Nat Shrine on Mount Popa.[16] The Nats are propitiated with respect to every important issue of life: birth, ordination, marriage, illness, death, prosperity in agriculture, taking a journey, undertaking a new venture. The Nat-goddess of the rice paddy is particularly powerful toward a good harvest or crop failure.

A number of different kinds of specialists (*hsaya*) are involved in spirit-propitiation. Women are particularly susceptible to possession by a Nat-spirit. The spirit, having entered her body, speaks through her, and thereafter she is considered his wife (*natkadaw*). The Natkadaw will be asked to dance at a spirit-ceremony; she serves as a medium through which a spirit is placated. The Nats particularly enjoy music, dance, and women. Also among the specialists are astrologers, curers of disease, and *pongyis*. The latter may also be astrologer and curer, but he is particularly important as one who chants Parittas which ward off evil spirits or call upon the help of the benevolent Devas.

Thai, Lao, and Cambodian animistic belief and practice follow much the same patterns as those of the Burmese, except that they have not produced anything comparable to the elaborate folklore relating to the thirty-six Nats. Among the Thai and Lao the most generally prominent spirits are the *phii:* the Phii of the House (*phii baan*), the Lord of the Area and Place (*Phra phuum caw thii*), the Phii Lord of the Field (*Phii caw thung*), the rice goddess, the Phii Guardian of the Village, and so forth. The Lord of the Area and Place (*Phra phuum caw thii*) who resides in a small house (patterned after the ceremonial hall of the *wat*) in the corner of the layman's yard is the counterpart of Min Mahagiri. The Phii of the House (*phii baan*), the spirit of a particular ancestor, serves a function comparable to that of the Mizaing-Hpazaing Nats.[17] As we have noted in connection with the ordination, the Shan of Burma, the Thai, Lao, and Khmer ritually honor the vital spirits of man (Thai-Lao:*khwan;* Cambodian:*pralung*). These spirits are recognized by the Burmese as the *leipbya*[18] but there are apparently no special rituals honoring them.

We have made mention of only a few of the spirits honored by Theravada Buddhists. Ritual occasions honor many others, some of which are strictly indigenous to particular localities of Southeast Asia and some of which originated in Brahmanical traditions of India introduced to Southeast Asia directly and through the Pali literature of Theravada Buddhism. The various *devatas* such as Indra, Brahma, and Yama who appear in the Pali Canon are invoked on almost every ritual occasion.

Any act of giving or participation in a ritual which honors the Buddha, from the simple devotion of offering flowers, incense, and candlelight before the Buddha-shrine or of reciting the auspicious marks of the Buddha while fingering beads, to the building or repairing of a monastery is merit-full.

No comparison can give an idea of the immortal value of the least offering. Whoever, with a pious soul, shall walk around the thats and other monuments containing relics, shall light candles, and bring flowers, whoever shall go on pilgrimage, will plant the deep roots of merits, keep out of Hell and go to Heaven.

That is why since our childhood we were taught to walk around the temples, . . . pledged ourselves to offer our hairs, our bones, our body and our heart. . . .

Expectantly we would await the feast days which, with a full moon in cloudless skies, would afford us the opportunity of working for a better life, thus showing some gratitude to our parents, e.g. by being well-behaved on the 6th month on the occasion of the Triple Revelation, . . .

By constantly hearing and repeating the Precepts in Pali. . . .[19]

Some acts are more merit-full than others. In general those acts which support the monk, the monastery, and the monastic way of life are most meritorious. Tambiah orders the acts of greatest merit among Thai Buddhists as follows, from greatest value to the least:

1. building a monastery
2. becoming a monk or having a son become one
3. giving money for the repair of a wat or for kathina gifts
4. daily food-offerings to the monks
5. observance of every uposatha (Wan Phra)
6. observance of the five precepts[20]

Nash finds similar priorities functional among the Burmese.[21] An increasing number of Theravada Buddhists see acts of social service and community development as meritorious.

The laity, especially women, make daily food-offerings to the household and yard spirits and to the monks — the former ensuring that the spirits continue to guard and prosper the family and its dwelling; the later to accumulate merit. They also make daily or frequent incense, flower, and candlelight offerings before the Buddha-image in the home and at the monastery. Four times each month on the moon-days (Uposatha) members of the laity (mostly women and older men) will go to the monastery to hear the monks chant, receive the precepts, and listen to a sermon by an elder Bhikkhu. On these occasions only a few of those present will understand the Pali chants. Some members of the laity will take eight precepts rather than five and remain at the monastery overnight keeping the basic discipline of the novice. Depending upon the education and the attitude of the preacher, the sermon may be simply a recitation of the Buddha-word or a directive commentary on some contemporary issue. Generally speaking, as with the Roman Catholic Latin mass, the importance of Uposatha to the layman lies not so much in edification by chanting and sermon but in the ritual itself and in being in the presence of and honoring the monk-priest. The Uposatha observance is always closed with a Bhikkhu indicating the merit gained by those who have taken part. It is widely believed that observance of the Uposatha protects one from attack by evil spirits.[22]

The rituals of the life cycle (concerning birth, death, marriage, house-building, etc.) performed in the home or as in the case of a funeral, at the monastery, bring the monk and layman together relative to family solidarity and prosperity. The monks 'bless' the laity and household spirits by their presence, chanting and sprinking of water, and in return they are fed and gifted by the laity.[23]

Closely associated with most of the life-cycle rituals and also performed on such occasions as ordination, illness, going on or returning from a journey, or honoring a guest is the Sukhwan or Bai Si ceremony. The Bai Si is performed to honor and protect an individual by calling together his vital spirits (khwan) and sealing them in his body. The ceremony centers around the bai si — a bowl of banana leaves shaped into several-tiered cones and bearing small balls of cooked rice at their tips. The officiant is usually a layman — former monk; but sometimes on occasion such as illness, a monk. He begins the ceremony by invoking the Buddha, Dhamma, and Sangha, putting the ritual in its proper context. Then he invites various of the gods, Indra (Sakka), Brahma, and so forth to take part and to bring wisdom, wealth, beauty, and fertility as may be appropriate to the person for whom the ceremony is being performed. In elaborate ceremonies there follows a circumambulation of the *bai si* by the officiant and others present holding lighted tapers. This done, the Khwan is offered food and called to return to the body of the recipient of the rite. The officiant draws a string around and over the body of the recipient, and then ties it on his wrist. This 'tying of the Khwan' ensures that it will remain in the body and is repeated by other participants in the ceremony.[24] In addition to the Sukhwan there are various other rituals to counteract disease. A group of monks may be invited to chant at the bedside of the ill or special incense, flower, and candlelight offerings may be made before one of especially powerful Buddha-images.

The spirit of the field and the spirit goddess of the rice paddy are propitiated by the farmer at critical points in the agricultural cycle. At the time of first plowing an altar is constructed in the corner of the field and food-offerings are made, usually by the farmer himself. When the rice is 'pregnant' (the grains are beginning to form) it is particularly important to honor the Rice Goddess that she may protect the field from malicious spirits and wandering men and animals who might trample the crop. With the Shan, Thai, Lao, and Khmer, this ritual is essentially a Sukhwan or Bai Si.

> The matter of making offerings to rice and to the Rice Goddess no doubt comes from the belief that various things have life; whether a human being or an animal or a plant, everything has something abiding in it which is called the khwan. If the khwan is not constantly present, the living thing dies. Rice is regarded as having life and a khwan, and so the khwan of the rice must be

treated in such a way as to cause it to remain present
and not slip away, for this might cause the rice not to
flourish or cause it to die.[25]

The rice and field spirits will also be honored at harvest
time. Depending on local custom and especially on how
good or bad the harvest, this may be a major, all-village festival or a relatively private affair. The monk or former monk
may be called upon to chant at any or all of the rice rituals.

Ordination and festival rituals are community affairs.
In the largest sense these celebrations cultivate and manifest
cultural unity at the village, regional, and national levels.
We have seen how an ordination brings merit not only to the
ordinand and his family but also to all who by their gifts
and presence participate. The power of ordination prior to
the rainy season is particularly directed toward heavy rains
and fertility of the soil.

As with ordination, the great festivals of the Buddhist
year are directed not only to honor and celebrate the Buddha, Dhamma, and Sangha, but also to occasion and celebrate prosperity in worldly affairs. Through these rituals the
merit-power of the Buddha and his monks is brought to bear
on the spirit-forces controlling the prosperity of the individual, the village, and the nation. The festivals common to all
Theravada Southeast Asians are those of the New Year
(April), Vesakha (May), Entrance into the Rainy-Season
(Vassa), Retreat (June–July), Leaving the Rain Retreat
(October), and Kathina (October–November); and the
major features of their celebration are everywhere the same.

The end of the old year, with the advent of the new, is
a time for summing up, cleaning up, and starting fresh. The
festival gives occasion for honoring the elders and the dead,
reflection on the deeds of the past, a symbolic cleansing or
washing away of bad deeds (demerit), an actual cleansing
of the monastery and Buddha-images, and a rededication to
Buddhist values. The new year appropriately begins at the
end of the dry season and the beginning of the new life in

nature. The pouring of water is not only an honoring of the Buddha, the elders, and the dead but also an offering for plentiful rain and prosperity in the days to come.[26] In Thailand, Laos, and Cambodia, the laity build sand 'pagodas' at the *wat* or on the bank of the river — each grain of sand represents a demerit, and placing the grains in the *wat* or letting them be washed away by the river symbolizes a cleansing from bad deeds. Bringing sand to the *wat* also serves to renew the floor of the compound. As is the case at all family and community rituals the monks chant blessing-formulas (*paritta*) and are offered food by the laity, and the laity renew their precepts. The Parittas are formulas held to have been preached by the Buddha for blessing and protection against evil spirits.[27] The following is frequently employed:

> Therefore may all blessings come to you, may all the devatas protect you with the power of the Lord Buddha. May good fortune be yours at all times.
> May all blessings come to you, may all the devatas protect you with the power of the Dharma. May good fortune be yours at all times.
> May all blessings come to you, may the devatas protect you with the power of the Order.
> May good fortune be yours at all times.[28]

It has also become custom throughout the area on New Year's Day to release captive animals — this is most appropriately done by the king and government officials.

Vesakha, which falls on the last full moon in May, celebrates the birth, enlightenment, and death of the Buddha, all of which occurred during the month of Vesakha — *punnama*. In celebration, the monks are offered special food and a larger number of the laity than usual participate in the Uposatha ritual. A special feature of Vesakha in Burma is the watering of pipal trees — the pipal being the tree under which the Buddha attained enlightenment. Thai, Lao, and Cambodian Buddhists give special honor to the Buddha by processing around the image carrying lighted candles and incense sticks at the conclusion of the Uposatha.

In the period from Vesakha to the entrance into the Rain Retreat (May–July) the villagers are especially concerned about the timely beginning of the heavy rains. Honoring the Buddha on Vesakha as well as ordaining young men to the monastic order for the coming Rain Retreat generates special power which is brought to bear in hope of rain. Thus, in Laos and parts of Northeast Thailand a rocket festival (Boun Bang Fay) aimed at rain-making is held on Vesakha itself. Other Thai Buddhists celebrate the same festival at the time of entrance into the Rain Retreat. Burmese Buddhists also have special rain-making rites at this time.[29] The rocket festival provides occasion for friendly competition between groups of monks and laymen in building and firing the rockets and occasion for general merry-making and courting among the young. The rockets are to anger the rain-spirits that they might hurl down torrents of rain and the villagers enjoy a good time before the heavy work in the fields and relatively austere living of the rainy season.

The beginning of the Rain Retreat is a time for monk and layman to commit themselves to a more rigorous adherence to the precepts. The monk must remain in residence at his 'home' monastery throughout the rainy season and intensify his study and meditation. In addition to making food-offerings to the monks, the laity present specially prepared candles to the monastery to burn throughout the retreat. In some villages and towns lay groups enter into a candle-making competition and prizes are awarded for the best candle. Thai, Lao, and Cambodian Buddhists perform a 'calling of the *khwan*' ceremony for the monks in order to ensure that all their vital energies are 'collected' for the coming retreat. In some areas rain-bathing cloths are presented to the monks. Everywhere there are special offerings to spirit-beings, especially to the guardian spirits of the village, transferring to them the merit of newly ordained monks in the hope that the spirits will protect the villagers and refrain from malicious deeds.

Strict Buddhists will not undertake celebrations such as marriages, ordinations, or Bai Si ceremonies during the Rain Retreat. There is one widely celebrated festival in Thailand, Laos, and Cambodia during the retreat — that held in September honoring the dead[30] — and one in Burma — that honoring the Taungbyon Brothers, particularly powerful spirits (Nats) of Upper Burma.

The end of the Rain Retreat is marked by food-offerings to the monks, and lengthy Uposatha. These ceremonies are the beginning of a month-long period of Kathina, the presentation of robes and other gifts to the monks (there is no one day for Kathina). The Kathina offerings to the monks are the most elaborate and most meritorious of their kind made during the Buddhist year — they provide the monk with his clothing and personal supplies for the next twelve months. The offerings are made by the community as a whole and almost every Buddhist participates. The participation of the king and government officials is widely publicized. In connection with the end of the Rain Retreat and the Kathina many Buddhists celebrate a festival of lights. Houses and monasteries are decorated and illuminated and in some areas the laity process around the Buddha-image with lights or float lighted candles on the water, commemorating the moment when the Buddha having gone to the Tusita heaven to preach the Dhamma to his mother descended again to the earth.

The month of Kathina is also a time of pilgrimage to famous shrines. Burmese Buddhists may go to the Shwedagon Pagoda in Rangoon or the Shwezigon Pagoda in Tagaung; Thai Buddhists, to Nakorn Pathom or the Shrine of the Buddha's Footprint (Phra Buddha Bat) at Saraburi. Offerings at such shrines are especially meritorious.

Many Buddhist villagers complete the yearly ritual cycle with a harvest festival in February or March, making offerings to the spirits accompanied by the prospering and protective chanting of the monks. The forces of nature are to be thanked in prosperity and propitiated in adversity.

There is a ritual rhythm to the life of the Theravada Buddhist. The yearly round of festivals is a ritual cycle co-ordinated with the agricultural cycle. All of the rituals of the Buddhist way, taken together, promote and express a symphony of life in which all of the various themes — the monk, the layman, the old, the young, the living, the dead, Buddha-power, and spirit-power — are constantly interacting in reciprocity. The monk and the layman are constantly 'meriting' each other. Parents and elders care for the young, performing protective rituals; the young male gives up the pleasures of worldly life, even his sexuality, to bring merit to his elders. The living share merit with the dead believing that the spirits of the dead will aid them or at the least re-frain from detrimental activities. The merit of the Buddha and the monk is offered to the spirits that they might prosper the layman's life toward continuation of his ability and capacity to praise the Buddha and support the monk.

Merit accrues to the individual in accordance with the extent to which he participates in a merit-full act. This may be understood by the sophisticated in terms of a thought, word, and/or deed occasioning a certain attitude and qual-ity of life within the person, and expressing an attitude and quality of life already present in a person. This may be un-derstood by the less sophisticated in a magical sense, as a thought, word, and/or deed materially conditioning forces in the cosmos which tend his existence in one direction or another. In accordance with either way of understanding, merit may be transferred from one person to another, as one person's action influences the attitude and quality of life of others around him or as material force is magically trans-ferred from one person's holdings to that of others. At the more sophisticated level it is difficult to comprehend how merit can be transferred from the living to the dead; but we must remember that the 'dead' are simply disembodied and are until (and perhaps even though) reincarnated close at hand.

The Way of the Laity

The devout Buddhist may speak only of the long-range effects of merit-making:

> In Laotian, "to do charity" is "hed boun" . . . i.e. acquiring merits for the next existence and if possible, to reach final Nirvana.[31]

Nonetheless, he is well aware of, but takes for granted, the manifold short-range implications of merit-making for the social, economic, and political patterns of his society — whether the merit-act is a food-offering to the monk or the construction of a hospital. In the village and to a lesser extent in the urban centers, social status, social mobility, the socialization process, and the economy are importantly conditioned by merit-making. The layman "has practised so as to conquer both worlds; he tastes success both in this world and in the next."[32]

We have indicated the high status and authority enjoyed by the monk and the former monk, not only with respect to ritual affairs but also with respect to the whole gamut of worldly concerns. This status is understood as merit-status. Kings, high government officials, and the wealthy are also considered to have great merit. In general, the more merit a man 'makes', the greater is his social status. The power and prestige which one holds are the result of past merit-making; likewise, the maintenance and enhancement of status depend on continued merit-making. Of course, the presently wealthy and prestigious have greater capacity to make merit than men of little wealth and power — we may say the former have greater social mobility than the latter. We must remember, however, that any male, of age, may become a monk thereby taking on the highest possible status without reference to economic or political power; and, considering the opportunity for an education and for a transvillage awareness open to a member of a nationally oriented monastic order, the monk may return to lay life with the potential for much higher status than he otherwise would have enjoyed. One's merit-potential is his social-mobility potential. In general, the male may enjoy greater social mobility than the female since he can become a monk;[33] the wealthy may enjoy greater social mobility than the poor since they can make greater merit.

Merit-making encourages particular patterns of socialization. Most merit-acts require social contact between individuals and between groups. The Uposatha and the rituals of the life cycle, ordination, and the great festivals require cooperative effort and promote family and village solidarity.

> The bonds of friendship among a number of groups are reinforced through activities associated with one of these ceremonies. Furthermore, the number and scale of these ceremonies is a source of pride to the villagers, furnishing them with a means of self-identification and expression of solidarity.[34]

In Burma merit-societies have come into prominence among the laity, especially in the urban centers. Such groups organize for specific services, food-offerings to the monks, pagoda-maintenance, recitations of scripture on the moon days and at festivals. The Sangha-Dana Soon-Laung Association of Rangoon sponsors food-offerings; the Shwedagon Cleaning Association periodically cleans the Shwedagon Pagoda area, and so forth.[35]

Merit-acts foster and express respect for the monk, parents, and elders, care for the young, and hospitality to the guest. Ordination provides a very positive means of promoting the separation of the male child from his parents as he comes of age; and, by bringing young men into a national organization (the Bhikkhu-Sangha) it encourages a trans-village regional and national outlook and involvement. Regional and national festivals promote a sense of regional and national identification and cultural unity. Last, but not least, merit-making provides a highly acceptable context within which to relax and 'let off steam'.

The implications of merit-making for the village and national economy have been much discussed by Buddhists and non-Buddhists concerned with economic development.

The extent to which surplus earnings are spent in merit-making significantly affects the village and national economies of Theravada Southeast Asia. Merit-making consumes resources of time, goods, and money which might be used otherwise. Pfanner reports:

> In one village of 150 houses in the Pegu District [Burma] during 1959–60 where the average annual net disposable family cash income was calculated to be about $200.00, a village total of $2,300.00 was spent in the two initiations and two alms-giving ceremonies during the year. . . . It was estimated by the writer that in the village mentioned above an average of from four to six percent of net disposable cash income available after production costs was spent for religious purposes.[36]

A 1953 survey by the Thai Ministry of Agriculture indicated that Thai villagers spent from 5 to 10 percent of their total cash income on merit-making.[37] Merit-acts also affect the village and national economy by distributing wealth. The wealthy expend more in merit-making and thereby distribute their wealth by 'gifting' and feeding other, less fortunate members of the society, laymen as well as monks. Cash donations in merit-making may find their way into consumption outside the merit context.

> Merit tends also to influence the composition of consumption in a re-distributive sense. The offerings of money or goods to priests or other families simply pass bits of income into other hands for consumption. The head priest may use some of the money given to the temple to buy a new record to be played over the temple loud speaker.[38]

The most significant innovation in lay Buddhist activity in recent times is the institution of formally constituted societies and associations under lay leadership for the promotion of the Buddha-Sasana ("Buddha-context"). These organizations are locally, nationally, and internationally oriented.

The Burmese Young Men Buddhist's Association founded in 1906 played a significant role as an instrument of Burmese anti-British nationalistic expression. Together with the YWBA (Young Women Buddhist's Association) founded in 1951 it continues strong in independent Burma promoting greater lay understanding and adherence to the Buddhist tradition and a variety of social welfare activities.[39] Burmese laymen have been most active of late in organized promotion of lay meditation. There are presently several hundred meditation centers throughout Burma such as the Sasana Yeiktha in Rangoon sponsored by lay-meditation associations.[40] The leading lay organizations in Thailand are the Buddhist Association of Thailand founded in 1933 under royal patronage and the Young Buddhist's Association founded in 1945. Both associations sponsor public lectures and publications for lay edification. With approximately fifty thousand members in fifty chapters throughout Thailand, the YBA most recently has directed its attention to the training of young people, especially university students, for village development work. Its membership has contributed money and medical supplies for the Bhikkhu-missions to the hill tribes.[41] The Buddhist Association of Thailand has come to function chiefly in relating Thai Buddhists to the World Fellowship of Buddhism.

Theravada Buddhist laymen, especially those of Ceylon, Burma, and Thailand, took the lead in founding the World Fellowship of Buddhism in 1950. The Fellowship was established to promote Buddhism as a world faith and more especially to foster better understanding and mutually beneficial interaction between Theravada and Mahayana Buddhists. Meeting every two years in a different country it has achieved not only some success in its primary purposes but also has served to enliven the lay and monastic Buddhism of each of the countries in which it has met. The Fellowship presently under the presidency of Princess Poon of Thailand has its headquarters in Bangkok.

VIII

Theravada Buddhism and Change: Looking to the Future

Perhaps the central function of a religion is to act as a cultural gyroscope, to provide a stable set of definitions of the world and, correlatively, of the self, so that both the transience and the crises of life can be faced with some equanimity by the society or person in question. It is this stability, continuity, and coherence provided by commitment to a set of religious symbols (or perhaps better to what they symbolize) that give religion such a prominent place in defining the identity of a group or person. Identity is a statement of what a person or a group is essentially and, as it were, permanently. Identity does not change except under severe pressure.[1]

BELLAH'S GENERALIZATION is obviously to the point in defining the role of Theravada Buddhism in Burma, Thailand, Laos, and Cambodia. In these countries the great majority of the people identify themselves with reference to Buddhist values. Their commitment to the Buddha, the Dhamma, and the Sangha provides stability, continuity, and coherence for their individual, social, and national existence. There can be

151

little doubt that this will remain true for some time to come. Throughout the area of Theravada influence in Southeast Asia, most urban as well as village-dwelling Buddhists continue to find the basic meaning of life in and through adherence to Buddhist-valued beliefs and practices of long standing. The mainstay of the Buddhist way of life, the Sangha, continues strong in numbers, in status in the eyes of the mass of the people, and in influence upon social, economic, and political activity.[2] In Thailand, Cambodia, and Laos official support of Buddhism is substantial (more so in the former two countries than the latter), and in Burma, albeit Buddhism is not officially established, the central government unofficially accords special status and support to the Buddha-Sasana. The Sanghas of Thailand, Laos, and Cambodia enjoy the strength of national unity and reasonably efficient administration. As a consequence, the level of adherence to the discipline on the part of individual monks is generally good. In all four Theravada societies the monks and the monasteries continue to play a significant role in elementary education.

At the same time, these societies are presently under great internal and external pressure for change — pressure toward rapid economic development, toward urbanization, toward education the content of which has been developed in non-Buddhist contexts. Theravada patterns of belief and practice are fundamentally attuned to a village environment, an agrarian society with relatively simple patterns of social, economic, and political interaction. Village Buddhists live in very close personal relationship with the earth and the natural environment in general. Their social life has traditionally been centered on the monastery. The recent rise of large towns and cities, increased efforts toward industrialization and diversification of the economy, the increasing availability of formal education in the humanities and sciences, and increased involvement of the central government in village affairs — these and other factors have combined to place considerable strain on traditional patterns. The city

(Bangkok, for instance) is not yet the American metropolis — it is rather more on the order of an overgrown village — and urban dwellers try to maintain "village" communities within it; but this is increasingly difficult. The monk finds the urban environment less personal than the village and with considerably more complex social, economic, and political patterns. He finds it requires more effort to maintain his discipline by reason of the sheer mass of people and the manifold diversions available. The wider range of occupations and consumer goods available make the lay life more inviting than in the village. The layman finds it impossible to adhere to the precepts and to honor the monk with the sense of belonging and clarity possible in the village. Public entertainments available quite apart from the monastery direct his attention away from the Buddha-context. Buddhist leaders are concerned that an increasing number of urban-dwelling Buddhists pay only superficial attention to traditional patterns — they are, so to speak, "Vassa-Kathina Buddhists" ("Christmas-Easter Christians"). Even in the village, it is increasingly the case that leisure time otherwise spent at the monastery listening to the monk or simply "soaking up" tradition is spent viewing movies or listening to the transistor radio. In both village and city increasing numbers of young people are receiving an education which broadens and sophisticates them without reference to the Buddhist understanding of life. Education toward a scientific understanding of man and his environment encourages a historically critical analysis of tradition and calls into question popular belief in spirits, especially as regards the cause and cure of disease and productivity in agriculture. National economic development schemes encourage investment and consumer spending to the neglect of merit-spending for temples, monasteries, and ritual celebrations.

Buddhist leaders are making an effort to cope with rapidly changing circumstances. The various local, national, and international lay Buddhist organizations which have come into being in the last few decades, especially in Burma and

Thailand, have served to increase the layman's awareness of the "outside world" and to sophisticate the layman's understanding of and participation in the Buddha-Sasana. Strong lay leadership whether emphasizing meditation (Burma) or social welfare merit-making is proving complimentary to monastic leadership and has encouraged greater public (as distinct from governmental) support in renewal of the Sangha and in social and economic development.

The most significant innovations in the Theravada Buddhist way have occurred with respect to the education of the monk. Concerned to prepare the monk not only to cope but also to maintain his leadership in an increasingly sophisticated and complex society, Sangha and government leaders, especially in Thailand and Cambodia, have moved to provide higher quality and greater breadth in monastic education, broadening the curriculum at the elementary level and providing opportunity for extensive studies in the humanities and sciences at the secondary and university levels. Leaders in Thailand, Laos, and Cambodia have tried with some success to promote among the monks themselves and among the laity a consciousness of the role of the Sangha in nation-building. The social service seminars for monks recently instituted in Thailand have had already a notable effect in fitting the monk for a more effective response to the social, educational, and economic needs of the people and for more effective leadership toward political integration of the country.

What of the future? What are the prospects for survival of the Buddhist way of life in the "modernizing" world? It is too simplistic and imperialistic[3] to conclude that survival depends upon modernization on the patterns of Western Europe, the United States, or the Soviet Union. Buddhists of Southeast Asia must forge a future in their own terms. Survival would seem at the least to depend upon stable government supportive of the Bhikkhu-Sangha, and a minimum level of worldly prosperity. These requirements in turn depend upon continued strong leadership in the Sangha, Bhikkhus and lay leaders increasingly well educated in the sciences and humanities and showing greater sophistication in their Buddhism, resistance on the part of Bhikkhu and layman to the depersonalizing tendencies of increased industrialization and urbanization, greater flexibility in agriculture, and a mass level direction of merit-spending to social welfare and economic development.

The Buddhist ideal is open to the future, positively concerned with worldly prosperity and promotive of Bhikkhu-leadership in temporal as well as spiritual affairs.[4] It is an individualistic ideal but not to the exclusion of a social ethic; nor is it world-denying. The individualistic self-discipline of layman and Bhikkhu crucially depends upon social interaction and temporal prosperity.

The way of the Buddha is essentially a way of the cultivation of individual moral character and insight in view of the suffering occasioned by the transiency of human existence. Human well-being is dependent upon individual internal self-discipline rather than manipulation of an external environment. A "good society" can only be defined as a collection of good individuals. Princess Poon Pismai Diskul of Thailand, president of the World Fellowship of Buddhism, in a recent public address summarized this point very well:

. . . it would be erroneous to assume that the Buddha's doctrine was personal to the exclusion of concern for human relationship and society at large.

The reason for emphasis upon individual development was founded upon the principle that the blind cannot lead the blind; or as the Buddha stated, "One, himself sunk in the mire of greed and delusion, cannot pull another out of that mire." One should first purify oneself to be able to show the way to others.

We can only have a better world when we first have better people. Fear, jealousy, ego-centrism, hatred, and greed are the original cause of human strife, be it petty crime or global war. Education, legislation and

arbitration, while useful countermeasures, will not suf-
fice to penetrate to the core of human motivation and
alter one's basic feelings. Buddhism is structured to do
just this. In fact such is its primary concern.[5]

In the light of Nibbana a good society is of only relative
value. But the Buddhist ideal does value a good society and
in fact demands it — social interaction in the world is the
instrument of a larger than worldly welfare. Implicit in the
ethic of individual self-discipline is a social, economic, and
political ethic. The "Middle Way" of the Buddha is neither
total renunciation of the world nor simple materialism, but
the way of the welfare of all beings through reciprocal
action according to their various kinds and conditions. The
Buddha taught reciprocal action permitting total renunciation for some and relative renunciation for others; and in
both instances, not renunciation of the world, but renunciation of desire, ego-involvement. The ideal is that the monk
and the layman give to each other and that their giving promotes *both* physical *and* spiritual well-being *both* here *and*
hereafter. The merit of the individual, whether he be monk
or layman, is dependent upon compassionate giving. The
monk gives up worldly affairs not for the sake of renouncing
the world but for the sake of renouncing desire. His discipline of self is a giving up the result of which is compassionate service of all suffering beings. Further, a man is not lost
short of leaving the lay life — for some to renounce there
must be those who do not so renounce. The monk has given
up worldly matters in favor of moral purity and wisdom
therethrough to provide a constant source of spiritual power,
a merit-field, for the larger society. He is a social-political-
economic conscience for the larger society, keeping the welfare state "on course" (to follow Bellah's "gyroscope" analogy). He can strive for purity and insight only as the layman
is committed to providing for his temporal needs, and this
very commitment is the layman's path to his own well-being.
The layman provides the essential means of the monk's re-

nunciation and in turn the monk inspires and guides the layman in acts of merit.

Acts of merit require worldly prosperity; indeed, prosperity here and prosperity hereafter are inseparable for
both the monk and the layman, the monk depending upon
the layman's prosperity for sustenance and the layman depending upon it for merit-action. Accordingly, scripture provides a positive, "balanced" stance on worldly wealth. The
layman's "work-ethic" is one of hard work, diligent striving
for wealth in accord with the five precepts and not as an end
in itself. It is an ethic dictating honest, nonviolent activity
the results of which are not dissipated by conspicuous consumption and riotous living — gambling, drinking, and sexual misconduct — and the results of which are used in promoting the welfare of other men, not only that of the monk
but that of the needy of this world and the spirits of other
worlds.

From the standpoint of this ideal, Theravada Buddhists
are not ill equipped for the future. The Bhikkhu in particular
may have special relevance to that future. Far from being
unproductive, an unnecessary drain on the economies of the
Buddhist societies of Southeast Asia, the individual monk
and the organized Sangha may be key forces for both stability and change. Given the high status and manifold role
of the monk in these societies a modern education may give
him more effective tools for doing for the society what he
has always done. Given a higher education in science and
the humanities, he may become a more effective preacher,
teacher, and counselor; given a knowledge of first aid and
modern medicines, he may become a more effective doctor;
and given training in administration and at least minimal
technical knowledge, he may become a more effective leader
in community development.

Though we are beginning to see this kind of Bhikkhu
in Southeast Asia, the ideal is far from actualized and the
obstacles to actualization are many. The temporary status
of many members of the Sangha is built into the whole life

style of Southeast Asian Buddhism, but it can become prob-
lematic if the monastic way fails to continue to attract a sufficient number of able men to long-term commitment. The
attractiveness of the monastic life depends upon effective
religious education among the laity and the continued high
status of the Bhikkhu. These in turn depend upon Bhikkhu-
education commensurate with the changing scene in the lay
society and nonmanipulative government support of Sangha.

With regard to education, it would seem minimally
necessary that the Bhikkhu be prepared to articulate the
Buddhist world view in relation to modern science and that
he interpret Buddhist values in the light of the changing
circumstances of lay life. Very little effort has been expanded
in this direction. Confrontation between Buddhist world
view and scientific world view may spell the doom of many
of the spirits whose movements are believed to occasion such
things as disease and crop failure, but sophisticated Buddhism should have no difficulty accommodating scientific
orientation to itself. Higher education in the social sciences
and humanities is required before Bhikkhu sermonizing and
counseling can amount to more than recitation of a text in
traditional language followed by traditional commentary.

Lao and Burmese Buddhists have only begun to provide
a higher education to the monk, and Buddhist communities
throughout the Theravada area are divided over what is
most needful in monastic education. Conservative laymen
and monks, notably those who support and follow the
Dhammayutika tradition in Thailand, Laos, and Cambodia,
feel that the primary emphasis in monastic education should
be placed on Pali-language and scriptural studies. They
argue that the welfare of the Buddha-Sasana depends crucially upon the purity and wisdom of the monk in accordance with the teachings and disciplines prescribed in scripture; the study of "secular" subjects encourages laxity in
both the keeping of the discipline and in the pursuit of insight through meditation. They point to instances in which
bright young men who might have provided needed leader-

ship in the Sangha, have, after completing their higher liberal studies, returned to the lay life where putting their education to use is materialistically rewarding. The liberal laymen and monks, on the other hand, argue that the continued welfare of the Sangha and Buddhism generally requires that the education of the monk keep abreast of that of the layman. The monk must understand the modern world if he is to effectively encourage living therein in terms of Buddhist values. As the layman becomes increasingly sophisticated through education, he will cease to support and rely on the monk who has no comprehension of the new circumstances in which the layman finds himself.

Both liberal and conservative have a point. While it appears mandatory that the Bhikkhu be educated to the changing scene, through this very education potential leaders of the Sangha may be more inclined to give up the Bhikkhu-life. "Secular" education for the Bhikkhu also makes for increasing strain between the elders and the "young bucks" of the Sangha. Those who presently exercise leadership in the Sangha are for the most part the older men who by age and attitude are least likely to undertake further formal education. Among these elder leaders one finds both instances of open-mindedness and closed-mindedness to youthful innovation. In a few instances there is evidence that young initiative has been squashed by accusations of communist sympathies.

The Bhikkhu's key status and role in Southeast Asia crucially depends upon government support without government control. Mutually beneficial Sangha-government relationships require a delicate balance, especially difficult to maintain in times of political turmoil. The power of the Bhikkhu lies in his passivity. The *pongyis* of Burma have not only sacrificed something in internal unity, but also have quite obviously suffered loss of status and power through active opposition to or support of one or another political party or government policy. Thai Bhikkhus "passively" participating in hill-tribe missions and development services are

perilously close to a very subtle form of government manipulation. While the various Thai, Lao, and Cambodian programs encouraging more effective social service on the part
of the monk have been initiated within the Sangha or by
Sangha and government jointly, these are programs which
are obviously useful to government by way of fostering
political integration and stability in the country from a particular political point of view.

The question of Sangha-government relations provides
the second line of conservative-liberal debate among Buddhist leaders. Conservatives admit that Sangha and government must work together for the welfare of the nation, but
argue that Sangha cannot do its part unless it be free to
exercise criticism of government policy in the light of uncompromised Buddha-truth. Liberals retort that under pressure for rapid change, Sangha and government cannot afford to work at cross-purposes. They submit that as long as
Sangha leaders determine that the monk is not engaging in
activity contrary to his discipline, the Bhikkhu-way will not
be compromised.

Buddhist leaders admit that most lay and monastic
Buddhists find themselves at the mercy of rather than in
control of the urban environment. The city in Southeast
Asia, like the city anywhere, promotes depersonalization and
alienation. The problem of the Bhikkhu's effectiveness in the
urban environment is not essentially unlike that of the minister, priest, or rabbi in Western societies, intensified by his
necessary passivity. The laity must lead in conquering the
city, yet lay "religious" education has not kept apace of lay
"secular" education. The layman's perception of a religious-
secular dichotomy is in fact symptomatic of the urban crisis.
If the education gap can be bridged, active lay societies may
be able to effectively perpetuate the village within the city
and assist the Bhikkhu to an urban style without loss of
essential values.

While it is not yet clear to this writer what types of
economic activity are necessary to future prosperity in

Southeast Asia, it appears certain that some new modes must be employed. The continued viability of the Buddhist ethic has been most questioned with respect to two particular types of economic activity — brief discussion of these may serve to suggest the potential of the Buddhist way.

The Buddhist ethic of nonviolence is functional relative to one's position as Bhikkhu, novice, or layman. The layman enjoys much greater leeway than the Bhikkhu. Even so, there is some evidence that this ethic may be an obstacle to certain means of greater productivity in agriculture and attempts at diversification of economy into animal husbandry. Pfanner and Ingersoll found among Burmese and Thai Buddhist farmers a general reticence to undertake any pursuit involving the killing of animals — in particular, the raising of livestock for slaughter. Nonetheless both researchers found farmers engaged in raising livestock, albeit with some trepidation. Pfanner reports an instance of violation of the prohibition on taking life in the interest of greater agricultural productivity which seems to illustrate the flexibility possible in such matters. Pfanner found Burmese groundnut farmers engaged in poisoning rats. They argued that the merit possible through the increased sale of groundnuts counterbalanced the demerit of killing rats in order to protect the crop.[6] The principle operative here appears applicable in general.

Lay Buddhists everywhere expend a significant portion of their income in merit-making activities such as ordinations, festivals, and temple-building. Continued high-level expenditure on such activities may prove detrimental to the savings and investment necessary to general economic development. Evidence is not yet available by which to prove or disprove this point. We have noted a significant trend toward new means of merit-making — the building of dispensaries, hospitals, schools, bridges, and so forth — encouraged by both Bhikkhu and lay leadership. Whatever the outcome of this trend, it is important to bear in mind that merit-spending of whatever sort *is* productive — productivity in the Buddhist context is not simply to be judged with reference to materialistic well-being to the exclusion of concern with mental and spiritual welfare in the short and long run. On the basis of studies among the Burmese, Melford Spiro has shown that, contrary to some evaluations, merit-spending is a rational rather than irrational activity, "appropriately productive, calculated to improve one's circumstances."[7] Thus, the Burmese do save and do invest and the question is one of incentive to make merit in one way rather than another.

This general and tentative estimate of the future prospects for the Buddhist way in Southeast Asia may be unduly optimistic. In any event, it is the opinion of the author that the problems facing Buddhist Southeast Asia are not simply the problems of a "traditional" society. Inasmuch as, at base, they are problems of temporal prosperity without spiritual deprivation, they are not essentially unlike those facing highly developed Western societies, and it would seem that Buddhism has as great a potential for human welfare in Southeast Asia as any alternative value-orientation.

Appendix

An outline of the Pali Canon: *Tipiṭaka* ("Three Baskets")

I. Sutta-pitaka ("Basket of Discourses") — the sayings of the Buddha and his disciples, grouped for convenience of memorization

    A. Digha-nikaya ("Collection of Long Discourses")

    B. Majjhima-nikaya ("Collection of Middle-Length Discourses")

    C. Samyutta-nikaya ("Collection of Kindred Discourses") — five groups of discourses, those in each group embodying teachings on the same subject and/or stories in which the same characters are prominent

    D. Anguttara-nikaya ("Collection of Gradual Discourses") — eleven groups of discourses in which successively onefold, twofold, threefold, etc., to elevenfold teachings are elaborated

    E. Khuddaka-nikaya ("Collection of Minor Discourses")

        1. Khuddaka-patha ("Little Readings")

        2. Dhammapada ("Verses on the Dhamma")

        3. Udana ("Solemn Utterances")

        4. Itivuttaka (" 'Thus it is said' Discourses")

        5. Sutta-nipata ("Collection of Discourses")

        6. Vimana-vatthu ("Stories of Celestial Mansions")

        7. Peta-vatthu ("Tales of Hungry Ghosts")

        8. Thera-gatha ("Verses of the Elders")

9. Theri-gatha ("Verses of the Nuns")
10. Jataka ("Lives")
11. Niddesa ("Exposition")
12. Patisambhida-magga ("The Way of Analysis")
13. Apadana ("Stories")
14. Buddhavamsa ("History of the Buddhas")
15. Cariya-pitaka ("Basket on Conduct")

II. Vinaya-pitaka ("Basket of Discipline") — rules and regulations for the monastic life
    A. Sutta-vibhanga ("Division of Rules") — the Patimokkha rules
    B. Khandhaka ("Sections")
        1. Mahavagga ("Great Series") — on ordination, Uposatha, Rain Retreat, food, clothing, medicine, and the like
        2. Cullavagga ("Small Series") — on judicial proceedings, ordination of nuns, dwellings, bathing, and the proceedings of the First and Second Great Councils
    C. Parivara ("Supplement") — summaries and classifications

III. Abhidhamma-pitaka ("Basket of Doctrinal Elaborations")
    A. Dhamma-sangani ("Enumeration of Dhammas") — on mental processes
    B. Vibhanga ("Distinctions") — on mental processes
    C. Dhatu-katha ("Discussion of Elements") — on mental elements
    D. Puggala-pannatti ("Description of Persons") — on persons at different spiritual levels
    E. Katha-vatthu ("Subjects of Discussion")
    F. Yamaka ("The Book of Pairs") — analysis proceeding from pairs of questions
    G. Patthana ("Book of Relations") — on causal relations

Notes

The number in brackets refers to the numbered works in the Bibliography. The source of a direct quotation and sources for additional information are indicated by the bracketed reference number.

INTRODUCTION

1. "The way (*vada*) of the elders (*thera*)"; historically, one of several sects collectively labeled Hinayana or "Lesser Vehicle" Buddhism as opposed to the Mahayana or "Greater Vehicle" Buddhism. Hinayana and Mahayana basically represent different responses to the historical Buddha. The Theravada-Hinayana definition of Buddhism was elaborated largely by monks who sought to follow the Buddha to enlightenment. The Mahayana definition was informed from the side of both popular devotion and meditative insight and emphasized the compassion of the Buddha for the salvation of all beings. Thus, in the Mahayana, enlightenment is only instrumental to a larger end. These variant responses to the Buddha were gradually distinguished in separate literatures and resulted in clearly distinct movements only outside India. From the late third century B.C. Theravada gathered its greatest strength in South India and Ceylon, later being exported therefrom to Southeast Asia. The Mahayana, promi-

nent throughout India down to A.D. 1000, gathered greatest strength in the North, from where it was exported through Central Asia to China as well as to Southeast Asia. The Theravada gradually came to dominate the Indianized areas of mainland Southeast Asia, while the Chinese Mahayana became the majority tradition of the Sinicized Vietnamese peoples.

2. Buddha-Sasana, literally, "the teaching of the Buddha"; as used by Theravadins it refers to all beliefs and practices inspired by the Buddha.

3. "In its essence and inner core, Buddhism was and is a movement of monastic ascetics." [49], p. 70. Unlike many others, Conze does consider the laity but in such a way as to make the layman purely instrumental to the monk rather than a full-fledged Buddhist in his own right. See also [61].

4. See [46], p. 167; and [64], p. 135 as examples.

5. Robert Slater is one of the few to recognize this: "In the study of great religious traditions there is always need to maintain a balance between regard for the written texts and for the living expression. To consult one without the other is to misinterpret both. What the Christmas stories in the gospels mean to Christians cannot be fully discerned if they are isolated from Christmas observance any more than the Jataka stories of Buddhism can be fully appreciated until they are read in the context of popular faith, with its drama and poetry. And what an entirely misleading impression of monastic Buddhism one might get from the Abhidhamma literature unless one has seen something of the life of a Buddhist monastery!" [99], p. 9.

CHAPTER I

1. [4], chap. 2, par. 9, pp. 26–27.

2. See Appendix for outline of the *Tipiṭaka*.

3. [56], chap. 33, v. 101, p. 237.

4. Historical-critical scholarship distinguishes early and late in the canon — that which is in all probability the original act and word of the Buddha and that which has accumulated around it over some five centuries. Significant portions of the Sutta (Discourses) and the Vinaya were in written form as

early as the fourth century B.C. Much of the Abhidhamma is quite late and was probably not part of the canon fixed by the monks of Ceylon in the first century B.C. See [71].

5. Buddhaghosa is also credited with having written several of the *Tipiṭaka* commentaries.
6. [9], p. 316.
7. [32], p. 5.
8. Ibid., p. 23.
9. Perfection in: almsgiving, keeping the precepts, renunciation, wisdom, courage, patience, truth, resolution, goodwill, and indifference.
10. The abode of the thirty-three gods.
11. [32], pp. 39–40.
12. Ibid., p. 43.
13. Enumerated beginning with "the blind received their sight."
14. [8], p. 151.
15. [32], pp. 45–47.
16. Explained below.
17. The dating of the Buddha depends upon the dating of King Asoka. According to the *Mahāvaṃsa* it was 218 years from the death of the Buddha to the consecration of Asoka. Theravada Buddhist scholars calculate the date of this consecration as 325 B.C., whereas critical historians date it 265 B.C. The Maha-parinibbana Sutta of the *Tipiṭaka* indicates that the Buddha was eighty years old when he died.
18. For example, having feet with level tread, thousand-spoked wheels on the bottoms of his feet, and long fingers and toes. See [10], pp. 137–38.
19. [32], p. 52.
20. [47], pp. 15–19.
21. [6], p. 101.
22. [32], p. 79.
23. Ibid., pp. 80–81.
24. Ibid., p. 81.
25. Literally, "discharge from a sore."
26. In particular, Sakka, King of the gods; and Mucalinda, King of snakes (*naga*) who coils himself around the Buddha's body as protection during a rainstorm. See [30], bk. I, chap. 3, p. 80.
27. [30], bk. I, chap. 5, p. 85.

28. [30], bk. I, chap. 24, sec. 5, p. 150.
29. [78], p. 98.
30. [4], p. 33.
31. [23], no. 5, v. 412.
32. [5], bk. I, sec. 319.
33. [7], vol. 2, disc. 86, sec. 98, pp. 284–85.
34. [4], pp. 36–38.
35. Ibid., p. 114.

CHAPTER II

1. [33], p. 126.
2. [33], pp. 117–22.
3. [33], p. 124.
4. [24], pp. 6–10.
5. [1].
6. My rendering, based on [70], p. 40.
7. See above, p. 16.
8. [34], p. 133.
9. [35], pp. 133–34.
10. [70], p. 40.
11. [22], p. 90.
12. [29], pp. 54–55.
13. [7], vol. 1, disc. 2, pp. 8–16; and [27], bk. III, chap. 5, secs. 9–10.
14. [70], p. 40.
15. [74], p. 43.
16. [47], p. 63.
17. This rejection of extreme asceticism is noteworthy in view of the tendency on the part of Western students of Theravada Buddhism to label its ideal as totally world-denying. The intent of the path is to understand and control the physical body and its processes, not to totally negate, suppress, and punish it.
18. See for instance, [7], vol. 1, disc. 44, sec. 301, pp. 362–64.
19. [11], p. 327.
20. [69], p. 3.
21. [11], pp. 344–45.
22. Ibid., p. 329.

23. Ibid., p. 329.
24. [7], vol. 1, disc. 30, secs. 201–5, pp. 248–52.
25. [13], pp. 84–86, italics mine.
26. [12], pp. 249 ff. [4] makes reference to yet one further absorption, the state of neither sensations nor conscious ideas, p. 52, and again, p. 115.
27. [13], pp. 88–93.
28. Thus, the texts dealing with meditation distinguish Samatha-bhavana ("concentration toward tranquillity of mind") and Vipassana-bhavana ("meditation toward insight into impermanence, unsatisfactoriness, and soullessness"). Tranquillity-meditation is an aid to insight-meditation. See [3], [85], and [50].
29. [36], p. 214.
30. [30], bk. I, chap. 5, pp. 84 ff.
31. [3], chap. 7, pars. 50–51 cites cases such as that of the frog reborn in a heaven as a result of hearing the Buddha's preaching.
32. She died seven days after his birth. [8].
33. [14], pp. 260, 265.
34. [37], pp. 289-91; and [15].
35. See [2], vol. 1, chap. 6, sec. 4, p. 194.
36. [14], p. 281.
37. Ibid., p. 280.
38. The Buddha perceives Yakkhas ("fairies, sprites, demons") dancing on the site where the city of Pataligama is to be built, showing the site to be an auspicious one. [30], bk. VI, chap. 28.
39. [38], pp. 313–14.
40. [26], p. 6.
41. [16], pp. 194–95.
42. [31], vol. 5, bk. V, chap. 6, pp. 148–49.
43. [26], p. 4. The Angulimala Paritta dispels evil by truth-speaking, [7], vol. 2, disc. 86, pp. 284–92.
44. [30], bk. VI, chap. 28, sec. 11, p. 103.
45. See discussion below.
46. Petavatthu, first story, quoted from [63], pp. 22–23.
47. [63], p. 29.
48. Peta-vatthu, secs. 4–5; quoted from [63], p. 28.

CHAPTER III

1. These terms cannot be satisfactorily translated by a single English word. Each of the words most frequently used in translation, "monk," "recluse," and "priest," conveys only something of the status and life of the Bhikkhu and Samanera. For ease of reading I shall use the term "monk" in reference to both Bhikkhu and novice, except where the context specifically requires distinguishing between them.
2. [17], p. 183.
3. [30], bk. I, chap. 11, p. 112.
4. [13], pp. 78–79.
5. [30], bk. I, chap. 12, secs. 3–4, p. 115.
6. There is an instance reported in which the Buddha permits the ordination of boys under fifteen years of age, so long as they are old enough to scare crows. [30], bk. I, chap. 51, pp. 204–5.
7. [30], bk. I, chaps. 49–51, pp. 201–5.
8. On one occasion, a snake (*naga*) desiring to become a monk assumed a human form and received ordination. His true identity was discovered when, as he slept, he returned to his snake form and the Buddha declared that a nonhuman could not be a member of the Sangha. [30], bk. I, chap. 63, pp. 217–19.
9. [30], bk. I, chap. 76, pp. 230–33.
10. [30], bk. I, chap. 25, sec. 6, p. 154. See bk. I, chap. 32, sec. 1, p. 179 for the same concerning the *acariya*.
11. The four cases of defeat require only one meeting of the community of monks.
12. [9], p. 317.
13. The Uposatha is occasion for the Bhikkhus to periodically prepare themselves toward continued observance of the discipline.
14. [30], bk. II, chaps. 3–4, pp. 241–47.
15. [31].
16. [30], bk. IX, chap. 4, pp. 268–73.
17. Novices need not observe this retreat.
18. [30], bk. III, chap. 4.
19. [30], bk. VIII, chap. 1, sec. 35, pp. 193–94.

20. [30], bk. VIII.
21. [34], p. 423.
22. [2], vol. 2, chap. 16, sec. 1, pp. 131–32.
23. [36], p. 418.
24. [2], vol. 2, chap. 16, sec. 4, p. 135. See also [7], vol. 3, disc. 151, pp. 342–45.
25. [2], vol. 2, chap. 16, sec. 3, pp. 133–34; and also here, the way to preach the doctrine.
26. [30], bk. VI, chap. 31.
27. [30], bk. VI, chap. 23.
28. [30], bk. I, chap. 11, sec. 1, pp. 112–13.
29. [27], chap. 4, sec. 3, v. 2, pt. I, pp. 230–31, italics mine.
30. Ibid.
31. Ibid., p. 232.
32. [17], p. 183.
33. Commanding spirits appears to be limited to the use of the Buddha-word as a Paritta (discussed above) for in the Brahmajala Sutta (Digha-nikaya, "Collection of Long Discourses") of the Pali Canon the Buddha cautions the Bhikkhus at length not to engage in "low arts" such as divining, exorcising, fortune-telling, fashioning charms, or setting lucky and unlucky days.
34. [27], chap. 4, sec. 8, v. 31, p. 155.
35. [17], p. 174.
36. [1], bk. IV, chap. 7, sec. 61, pp. 73–77; also bk. V, chap. 5, sec. 43, p. 39.
37. [1], bk. IV, chap. 7, sec. 61, pp. 73–77.
38. [18], p. 182.
39. [17], pp. 174–75.
40. [17], pp. 180–81.
41. [1], bk. IV, chap. 7, sec. 62, pp. 77 ff.
42. ". . . the four channels for the flowing in of great wealth are these: abstinence from looseness with women, from debauchery in drinking, from knavery in dice-play and having friendship, companionship and intimacy with the good." [1], bk. V, chap. 23, sec. 227, p. 190.
43. [1], bk. VIII, chap. 6, sec. 54, pp. 187–89.
44. [1], bk. X, chap. 10, sec. 91, pp. 123–24.
45. [1], bk. V, chap. 4, sec. 41, pp. 37–38.
46. [1], bk. IV, chap. 6, sec. 60, p. 73.

47. [7], vol. 3, disc. 142, pp. 300–305.
48. [30], bk. VI, chap. 28, sec. 5, p. 100.
49. [1], bk. IV, chap. 7, sec. 61, p. 77.
50. [19], p. 62.
51. [27], pt. II, chap. 4, sec. 5, v. 37, pp. 41–42.
52. [19], pp. 63–64.
53. [20], p. 88.
54. [3], chap. 13, par. 54, p. 460.
55. [27], pt. II, bk. VII, chap. 3, sec. 30, p. 323.
56. [19], pp. 62–63.
57. [21], p. 218.
58. See above, pp. 36–37.
59. [21], pp. 218–29. The King Vessantara birth of the Buddha, being the Future Buddha's last birth, even suggests that a great king may, like Vessantara, be on the verge of Buddhahood.
60. [4].
61. [19], pp. 65 ff.

CHAPTER IV

1. [56], [92], [94], [144], and [129].
2. The dates of kings will always indicate period of reign.
3. [56], chap. 1, vv. 21 ff. *thupa (stupa)* — "a memorial mound."
4. [56], chaps. 3, 4, and 5.
5. [56], chap. 12, vv. 3–8, p. 82.
6. The tree under which the Buddha attained enlightenment.
7. E.g., by King Mahasena (A.D. 334–361) and Tamil invaders in the first century B.C.
8. Sinhalese and Burmese Buddhists consider this gathering to be the Fourth Great Council of Bhikkhus since the death of the Buddha; the Thai take it as the fifth council, the fourth having been the gathering of monks at the constitution of the Mahavihara under King Devanampiya Tissa.
9. For the history of Buddhism in Ceylon see [39], [72], and [73].
10. [94].
11. [92], pp. 41–42.

12. The Thai venerate a Buddha-footprint at Saraburi, and the Lao, one at Luang Prabang.
13. [92], pp. 11 ff.
14. [132], pp. 1–2; [131]. [65], p. 42 argues that Suvannabhumi was somewhere in present-day Indonesia. [59], pp. 15, 18, and [48] are noncommittal on the matter.
15. [56], chap. 12, vv. 52–54, pp. 86–87.
16. [56], chap. 5, p. 42.
17. [56], chap. 5.
18. I follow [52] and [51]. B. G. Gokhale argues that Asoka was not only an ardent Buddhist layman but that ". . . Asoka's zeal transformed Buddhism from a small sect into a world religion. . . ." He further argues for the historicity of the monk-missions which the chronicles assert Asoka urged. [57], p. 58.
19. [94], pp. 47 f.
20. The Thai chronicles maintain that Anoratha conquered Nakon Pathom rather than Thaton.
21. [59], pp. 147 ff.
22. Ibid., pp. 164–65.
23. [72], p. 62.
24. [132], p. 22.
25. [129].
26. The Sihing (Sinhala=Sinhalese) Buddha is one of three famous Buddha-images of Southeast Asia, all, according to tradition, fashioned in Ceylon and possessed of special powers. The Sihing image was taken to Chiengmai from Sukhodaya where it was installed at Wat Phra Singh (Sihing) around 1400. Some Thai claim that the original image is now in the national museum having been brought to Bangkok from Chiengmai in 1796. Northern Thai Buddhists hold that the original is still in Wat Phra Singh and that the Bangkok image is one of two replicas made at Chiengmai.

The Emerald Buddha, now in Bangkok and considered the chief symbol of official Buddhism in the Kingdom of Thailand, was discovered at Chiengmai in 1436. According to tradition it was made in Ceylon in the third century A.D. by Sakka himself. In the mid-sixteenth century Settatirat took the image from Chiengmai to Vientiane and having established himself there installed the image in Wat Phra Keo. The Thai took the image from Vientiane when they devastated the city in 1778.

    In the same conquest the Thai also took from Laos the Prabang Buddha brought from Phnom Penh to the present site of Luang Prabang in the mid-fourteenth century. King Mongkut of Thailand returned the image to Luang Prabang in 1868 and it now resides in that city at Wat Mai, the chief royal monastery of the kingdom.

27. [48], p. 208.
28. Ibid., p. 178.
29. [112], pp. 24–25.
30. See footnote 26 above.
31. [155], p. 42.
32. [59], p. 626.
33. [100], p. 160.
34. [152].
35. [59], p. 261.
36. [132], pp. 27–28.
37. [59], p. 175.
38. Since the introduction of the Sinhalese ordination line in the late twelfth century there had been tension between the Sinhala and the older Thaton or Maramma orders.
39. After the place of reordination in Ceylon.
40. One party of monks insisted on wearing the robe off one shoulder (*ekamsika*) while the other held to the covering of both shoulders (*parupana*); Bodawpaya decreed in favor of the latter, deeming this pattern the more ancient. See [97].
41. [97]. [53] says four Sangharajas and four assistants to them.
42. For Burmese Buddhists this is the Fifth Great Council since the death of the Buddha.
43. The Constitution Bill and the State Religion Promotion Bill.
44. The four cases of defeat, see pp. 50–51 above.
45. [133].
46. [132], p. 26.
47. The fourth called by Devanampiya Tissa (third century B.C.); the fifth — the writing down of the Pali texts — under Vattagamini (first century B.C.); the sixth under King Mahanama in the time of Buddhaghosa (fifth century A.D.); the seventh under King Parakramabahu (twelfth century A.D.).

48. [132], pp. 30–31.
49. See below, Chapter V.

CHAPTER V

1. [17], p. 183.
2. [86], pp. 193–94.
3. [85], pp. 41–84.
4. Ibid., p. 72.
5. [2], pt. IV, chap. 40, sec. 10, p. 187. Recited regularly in Thai rituals; see [130].
6. [95], p. 321. This language is used also with respect to the king, the Buddha, and certain of the gods.
7. In Theravada Southeast Asia it is considered improper to point the sole of the feet toward any other person, but especially the monk. The basis for this custom would seem to be the belief that the soles of the feet are most vulnerable to evil spirits or most in contact with the earth where such spirits often reside.
8. [120], p. 244.
9. [83], p. 132; for comparable comment on the status of the Bhikkhu in Thailand and Cambodia see [96], pp. 351–52 and [40], p. 177.
10. "Monasteries."
11. "Monasteries"; the basic meaning of the word *kyaung* is "school" — until recent times schooling was provided only in the monastery. Now that schooling is available outside the monastery, the monastery-school is often designated the *pongyi -kyaung* ("monk-school").
12. The figures for Thailand, Laos, and Cambodia were provided me in 1967 by the Department of Religious Affairs, Thailand; the Ministry of Cults, Laos; and the Ministry of Cults, Cambodia. See also [148], p. 1; [122], p. 52; and [119], p. 64. Estimates only are available for Burma and these run from 80,000 to 800,000. Tinker notes a 1953 estimate of 100,000 by the Social Planning Commission of Burma as a "distinct underestimate" and prefers the 800,000 used in a government statement in Parliament, 1954. [106], p. 168. Slater and Pfanner estimate 1 percent and 1.3 percent of the total population respectively — I follow them. [99] and [95]. The

number of Kyaungs in Burma is a rough estimate, following Hobbs who reported 17,500 monastic schools in 1952. [84], p. 81. According to the *Area Handbook for South Vietnam* there are approximately 500 Theravada monasteries in the Southern Mekong Delta area. [77], p. 181.

In Burma and Thailand there exists an order of nuns. The number of nuns is relatively small — there are about 10,000 in Thailand at the present time. Women are not encouraged to take up the monastic life and those who do are largely either orphaned girls, young women who have "lost at love," or aged widows. While the nun is respected by the laity, she by no means enjoys a status comparable to that of the monk. She follows a discipline comparable to that of the novice.

13. The government of Thailand grants three months' paid leave to civil servants who desire to enter the monastic order.

14. David Pfanner reports that all males in the villages of Pegu District in Lower Burma spend some time as novices in the monastic order. [40], p. 83.

15. May Ebihara reports 75 to 80 percent in his villages of Cambodia. [40], p. 183; Michael Moerman reports that only 30 percent of the males of Ban Ping, Thailand, over fifteen years old have been ordained. [40], p. 139.

16. [120], pp. 250–51.

17. In 1965 there were over 97,000 temple boys (*dekwat*) serving *wats* throughout Thailand. [126].

18. To be discussed below, Chapter VI.

19. For example, the cost of two novitiate ceremonies in Mayinywa village, Burma, in 1960 was 5,072 kyats ($1,000) and 2,262 kyats ($475) respectively. [95], p. 352.

20. Very often the candidate for ordination is sponsored by a person other than a member of the immediate family and preferably belonging to the same kin group. The sponsor bears the major burden of the cost of the ceremony and receives a major portion of the merit. This is the beginning of a lifelong relationship between the sponsor and the candidate.

21. [30], bk. I, chap. 63, secs. 1–5, pp. 217–19.

22. Recall Mucalinda, the seven-headed Naga who coiled himself under and around the Buddha a short time after enlightenment, sheltering him from the rain.

23. Blackening the teeth of the 'Naga' is based on a popular legend of a king who having married a *nagi* (fem. of *naga*) who had taken the form of a beautiful woman had to lacquer her teeth to keep her from reverting to her serpent form. [117], pp. 23–24.

24. [80], pp. 116 f.

25. Lao:*baci;* Khmer:*baysei.* The Khmer also call the ceremony *bay pralung.*

26. [80], pp. 116–17.

27. [40], p. 121.

28. In the cities in recent times a car is sometimes used.

29. See [114], pp. 406–8, for a vivid description of the traditional procession in Cambodia.

30. See Chapter III, p. 50.

31. I would not press this interpretation so far as does Paul Lévy in [66], but Lévy's theory provides an interesting thesis for further study. Examining ordination practices in the Theravada and Mahayana traditions in the light of their ancient roots and aspects of the Western mystery religions, he views the ordinand as a sacrificial victim promoting the liberation of those who perform the sacrifice. Lévy points out that when the ordinand receives his robes from his spiritual guide he is hunched down in an 'embryo-position', his hands and neck tied together with the sash of his monastic attire; after being shaved and ritually bathed, he may be taunted and beaten or, more likely, simply teased by other novices about the way he wears his robe or carries his bowl. He is symbolically killed and achieves new birth in final acceptance into the circle of monks.

"There is no disputing this sacramentalising of the pseudo-victim. It is proved by the way in which he is set up on high and by the veneration which even the oldest monks accord to him. 'All honour to the latest arrival!' The fresh bloom of his passion and of his consecration make him especially precious; the body of the Law is renewed by him, incarnate in him. . . .

"In my opinion it has not been sufficiently stressed that Buddhism is solidly based on a rigid system of gifts and exchanges: gifts of food and of a thousand and one material objects; gifts of human creatures who take the place of sacrificial victims. The benefits anticipated from the gifts by their givers concern in particular prolonged survival and eternal bliss." [66], pp. 100–108.

32. See [93] and [82], p. 353.
33. In Thailand one may do this only three times [154], p. 130.
34. Wat Borvornives is Dhammayuttikanikaya and Wat Mahadhatu is Mahanikaya.
35. "Dhamma-scholar."
36. Pali: Parinna ("exact knowledge").
37. This figure includes 15,000 laymen; the Nak-Dhamma course of studies is now open to the laity.
38. [126].
39. [100], pp. 66–71.
40. Ibid., pp. 226–28.
41. [124], p. 443.
42. [110], p. 96.
43. [134], p. 10, italics mine.
44. Ibid., p. 14.
45. According to Winston King, a Buddhist Sangha University was founded in 1955 in Rangoon with the intention of developing a high school and university curriculum toward the Bachelor of Arts degree, [86], p. 217. I have no information on the curriculum or the present status of this institution.
46. In Burma these ranks are recognized by the titles, Pongyi and Sayadaw; however, in recent times it appears that *pongyi* is popularly applied to any monk and *sayadaw* has come to refer to any abbot of a *kyaung;* in Cambodia the ranks are called Thanah Ouckram and Reachea Khanac.
47. See above, Chapter III, pp. 50 ff.
48. Claiming greater spiritual insight than he has actually achieved. These are the four cases of defeat, see pp. 50–51 above.
49. [93].
50. [100], chap. 6.
51. Ibid., pp. 190–91.
52. The National Registration Act of 1949 required all citizens of Burma to be registered and carry identification but opposition from leading *sayadaws* made registration of the monks impossible. Ibid., p. 216.

53. Ibid., pp. 217–20.
54. Ibid., pp. 281 f.
55. Ibid., p. 286.
56. The festival of the last full moon in May celebrating the Buddha's birth, enlightenment, and death. See Chapter VII for a description of the celebration.
57. The festival of supplying the monks with robes and other necessities following the rainy-season retreat. See Chapter VII.
58. See [125], foreword.
59. See [121].
60. Ne Win recently held an elaborate *shinbyu* ceremony for his son.
61. [76], pp. 127–28.
62. [105], p. 23.
63. There is a third group, the Dvara Order, but its numerical size and distinctiveness do not appear worthy of note. Its name apparently derives from the fact that the monks prefer to use "the expressions *kaya-dvara, vaci-dvara, mano-dvara* (the doors of body, tongue and mind) instead of *kaya-kamma, vaci-kamma,* and *mano-kamma* (actions of the body, tongue, and mind)." [41], p. 121.
64. It is possible that the founding of the Shwegyin was influenced by the Dhammayuttika movement in Thailand. Or, it may be that the Shwegyin like the Dhammayuttika was independently influenced by the Buddhism of Mon monks residing in southern Burma and southern Thailand.

CHAPTER VI
1. [30], bk. I, chap. 11, sec. 1, pp. 112–13.
2. [138], p. 5.
3. Ibid., see appendix, pp. 145–46; see [154], chap. 3 for a representative selection of Suttas recited on these occasions.
4. The petitions of the monk in lighting candles, and incense, the praise of the Buddha, and the taking of refuge before the Buddha-image — ideally acts of meditation toward self-discipline, expressions of confidence in the Dhamma and Vinaya as a true way — may appear to the non-Buddhist as acts of worship inconsistent with the stated belief that the Buddha was a man who lived and died and is no more.

5. See [25] and [154].
6. [40], p. 142.
7. At domestic ceremonies the string may be attached to the house of the spirit (guardian of the house and land) thereby conveying merit-power to him.
8. A government Department of Education was formed in 1887. [149], H1.
9. [121], appendix II, table 5.
10. [105], p. 23.
11. [95], p. 328.
12. [40], p. 86.
13. [99], p. 23; also [105], p. 23.
14. [40], pp. 62–63.
15. [40], p. 166.
16. [140], p. 75.
17. Ibid., pp. 78–81.
18. [76], p. 89.
19. See [100]; [121], pp. 49 f; and [119], pp. 72–73.
20. [76], pp. 102–3.
21. [121], p. 145.
22. In 1967 there were twenty-one monks in the former, and thirty-four in the latter.
23. An expert in mental development following the Abhidhamma Pitaka of the Pali Canon.
24. The abbot of Wat Phra Singh had donated 700 baht toward the building of a school.
25. [126].
26. Fifty, the first year; seventy, the second.
27. [115], Janvier–Mars, 1965, p. 169.
28. [115], Janvier–Mars, 1965, pp. 51–52.
29. Sangkum Reastr Niyum ("People's Socialist Community"), the political party of Sihanouk.
30. [115], Janvier–Mars, 1966, pp. 51–57.
31. The Union Buddha Sasana Executive Council and the Union Buddha Sasana Council, nongovernmental lay groups formed in 1950 by the Ministry of Religious Affairs under the Buddha Sasana Organization Act, undertook support of a *pongyi* mission to the non-Buddhist hill-tribes peoples. The missions were organized by private groups such as the All-Burma Buddhist Association and the Society of the Propagation of

Buddhism. On September 21, 1959, the *New Times of Burma* (formerly *Burmese Review* and *Monday New Times*) reported that 124 monks were in the field, 122 schools had been established, and 131,322 'converts' had been made. In the same year the Society for the Propagation of Buddhism ordained 41 Nagas, Kachins, Shans, and Chinese at Myitkyina. The ceremony was attended by numerous officials including the Minister of Religious Affairs (*New Times of Burma*, Nov. 21, 1959). See also [100], pp. 154–55. I have no information on the status of this program since 1959.

32. [96], p. 349.
33. See [100].

CHAPTER VII

1. [27], chap. 4, sec. 8, v. 31, p. 155.
2. [17], p. 174.
3. [40], p. 73.
4. A layman formally designated to assist in rituals and aid the monks in the administration of monastery affairs.
5. [40], p. 185.
6. [40], pp. 155–56.
7. [17], p. 184.
8. See [141], p. 23; [40], p. 187; [99], pp. 22–23; and [40], p. 68.
9. There is disagreement among scholars as to the status of spirit-worship and its relation to Buddhism in Theravada Southeast Asia. A. C. Bouquet, a generalist, writing on Buddhism without adequate awareness of patterns of life in Southeast Asia and no doubt echoing writers such as Sir R. C. Temple [104], concludes that the mass of the people of Burma are not Buddhist at all but animists:

> Hinayana is still "the little vehicle," because it does not and cannot appeal to the masses of any population. It is a creed for a minority. It is true that it is the Buddhism of Burma and Ceylon. But anyone who knows these countries is well aware that the real popular faith of their peoples is not Hinayana but a thinly veiled animism. [46], p. 167.

A number of scholars who have made village studies in Theravada Southeast Asia argue that Buddhism and spirit-worship are two distinct belief-systems. They maintain that most Buddhists are also animists and that the two systems somewhat "comfortably" coexist, Buddhism dominantly providing the larger value context and dealing particularly with a favorable conditioning of the next life, and animism providing the means of dealing with the mundane affairs of this life. See [40], p. 190; and pp. 132–33; and [147]; and [103]. Manning Nash takes this point of view in such a way as to bring him very close to the fully integrated point of view I have taken above:

> Buddhism and the Nats are not in conflict and nowhere in contradiction, but work mutually to give the villager a constant and rather clear view of the remoter ends of human existence while allowing him to deal with daily problems. [90], p. 291.

It is important to recognize that historically several different belief-systems (Brahmanism and Mahayana Buddhism as well as Indian and Sinhalese Buddhism and local animism) have been distinguishably functional among the Southeast Asian peoples who are now Theravada Buddhists. But it must also be recognized that Theravada Buddhism came to Southeast Asia already 'Brahmanized' and replete with all kinds of spirit-beings and had no difficulty in fully assimilating the Brahmanistic and animistic beliefs and rituals previously popular. Kenneth Landon suggests only one of the ways in which assimilation had taken place:

> For most of the people in Siam, Buddhism has provided, among other things, new ways of controlling evil spirits. A Buddhist amulet or a necklace of metal cylinders containing Pali sutras may be hung about the neck for protection. If one becomes ill, some lustral water made potent by the chanting of monks may be sprinkled on him to drive out the spirit. In cases of severe illness a chapter of monks may be invited to chant for the recovery of the person. It is a rare child in Siam, even in modern times, who does not wear a charm or amulet at

some time or have lustral water poured over him. [62], p. 30.

See [139], [146], [85], and [81] for approaches similar to the one I have taken.

10. The identification of Sakka with Thagyamin indicates one of the ways in which Nat worship was assimilated to canonical Buddhism.
11. [80], p. 78.
12. Ibid., pp. 63–65.
13. The coconut is replaced at the birth of a child or a death in the family. [40], p. 119.
14. Ibid., p. 122.
15. *New Times of Burma*, April 13, 1951, quoted in [100], p. 173.
16. [100], p. 176.
17. See [147] on Thai spirits. The spirits of Cambodia are variously known as *chmniang pteah* ("household spirit"), *meba* ("ancestral spirits"), and *neak thaa* ("spirits of the land, village, the rice, and other natural phenomena"). See [40], p. 189 and [119], pp. 75–76.
18. See [75], p. 121.
19. [120], p. 243.
20. [146], p. 69.
21. [91], p. 116:

    1. to build a pagoda
    2. to give a shinbyu (act as sponsor for a novice monk)
    3. to build a monastery (and donate it to a monk)
    4. to donate a well or bell to a monastery
    5. to give a hsungwe (to feed a group of monks)
    6. to feed and give alms to monks
    7. to feed and give hospitality to laymen

22. [40], pp. 132–33.
23. See discussion of these rituals in Chapter VI.
24. See [75].
25. [143], p. 25.
26. In parts of Burma and Laos the young people have a general water-throwing melee–sprinkling water for rain would seem to be a kind of sympathetic magic.

27. See discussion of these in Chapter II.
28. [154], p. 243.
29. [40], pp. 103–4.
30. [146], pp. 73–74; [116], pp. 47–56.
31. [120], p. 243.
32. Sigalovada, quoted above.
33. Kirsch suggests that the Thai Buddhist male tends to seek status either through becoming a monk, pursuing a career in government service, or both. He argues that since the king, at the top of the political structure, as well as the monk belongs to the highest class of human beings (the 'ong' class), those who join government service as well as those who join the monastic order enjoy something of 'ong' status. Male gravitation toward the monastic life or government service leaves the realm of commerce open to the female, and, in fact, Thai women are prominently engaged in commercial activities. [139], pp. 206–8. See also Kirsch, "The Thai Buddhist Quest for Merit," unpublished paper, 1969; [142], pp. 384–99; [135] and [101] for discussion of the status and mobility implications of merit-making.
34. [95], pp. 397–98, speaking specifically of *shinbyu* and *kahtein*.
35. [82], pp. 335 f.
36. [96], p. 348.
37. [149], D41.
38. [96], p. 356.
39. [108] and [82].
40. See [82] and [85], p. 225.
41. Based on my interviews, 1967. See also [55].

CHAPTER VIII

1. [43], p. 173.
2. Sangha and government leaders note a decrease in Sangha membership as a percentage of the total population and a decrease in the number of career commitments to the Sangha over the last few decades, but this is not alarming; the total number of monks has steadily increased (at least in Thailand, Laos, and Cambodia) and a larger number of short-term monks are remaining five to ten years in the order to

complete their education. I am relying on conversations with Buddhist leaders in late 1967. Statistics available on the Thai Sangha, 1960–65, do bear out the generalization — Sangha membership in 1960 was 255,539 as compared to 261,377 in 1965. The total number of monks in 1960 was .97 percent of the total population, whereas the total number in 1965 was .85 percent of the total population.

3. The terms "modern" and "traditional" are frequently used in opposition as if they did not require definition relative to particular circumstances. Consequently, development analysts may assume they are proceeding with respect to generally accepted standards when in fact they are simply pitting one way of life against another. This is a very subtle form of cultural imperialism. Gunnar Myrdal, who takes great pains to criticize development experts for their lack of adequate awareness of South Asian traditions, nonetheless without showing adequate awareness on his own part concludes:

> Religion should be studied for what it really is: a ritualized and stratified complex of highly emotional beliefs and valuations that give the sanction of sacredness, taboo, and immutability to inherited institutional arrangements, modes of living, and attitudes. . . . The writer knows of no instance in present-day South Asia [he includes Southeast Asia] where religion has induced social change. Least of all does it foster realization of the modernization ideals. . . . [67], vol. 1, p. 103.

Religion so defined cannot but be in conflict with modernity and the conflict must be even greater when, as by Myrdal, South Asian religion is set over against modernization ideals which are defined in terms of Western secular values.

4. This conclusion stands in contradiction to the generalizations of at least two eminent students of Buddhism. Max Weber concludes:

> At the opposite extreme from systems of religious ethics preoccupied with the control of economic affairs within the world stands the ultimate ethic of world-rejection, the mystical illuminative concentration of authentic ancient Buddhism. . . . There is no path leading from this

only really consistent position of world-flight to any economic ethic or to any rational social ethic. [79], pp. 266–67.

More recently, Joseph Kitagawa comes to a similar conclusion:

> In the main, Buddhism traditionally has been characterized by a quietistic view of Nirvana or Nibbana, a static understanding of the givenness of the environment, and a negative attitude toward life, world, and history. The leading motif of traditional Buddhism was its emphasis upon the transiency and meaninglessness of everything in this world, so that the path of the Buddha was sought in liberation from attachment to tangible forms and values in the phenomenal world. [61], p. 7.

Weber and Kitagawa draw their conclusions on too narrow a view of the Buddhist ideal and apparently without awareness of patterns of life in Theravada Southeast Asia.

5. [151].
6. [96], p. 346.
7. [101], pp. 1163–73.

Bibliography

The bibliographical listings are arranged in categories: A. Scriptures in Translation; B. General; C. Burma; D. Cambodia; E. Laos; F. Thailand. Within each category the sources are arranged alphabetically. Each work is given a reference number in brackets. This bracketed number has been used in the Notes to indicate the source of a direct quotation or sources for additional information.

A. Scriptures in Translation

[1] *Book of the Gradual Sayings (Anguttara-Nikaya)*. Translation Series. Vol. 1 (1951), vol. 2 (1952) F. L. Woodward, trans.; vol. 3 (1952), vol. 4 (1955) E. M. Hare, trans.; vol. 5 (1955) F. L. Woodward, trans. London: Luzac and Co., 1960.

[2] *Book of the Kindred Sayings (Samyutta-Nikaya)*. Translation Series. Vol. 1 (1951), vol. 2 (1953) T. W. Rhys Davids, trans.; vol. 3 (1954), vol. 4 (1956), vol. 5 (1956) F. L. Woodward, trans. London: Luzac and Co., 1956.

[3] Buddhaghosa, Bhadantacariya. *The Path of Purification (Visuddhimagga)*. Translated by Bhikkhu Nyanamoli. 2d ed. Colombo, Ceylon: A. Semage, 1964.

Bibliography

Buddhist Suttas. Translated by T. W. Rhys Davids. Unabridged and unaltered republication of vol. 11 of *The Sacred Books of the East,* 1881. New York: Dover Publications, 1969.

[4]   Maha-parinibbana-sutta.

Burlingame, E. W., trans. *Buddhist Legends.* Harvard Oriental Series. Cambridge: Harvard University Press, 1921.

[5]   Dhammapada Commentary.

Chalmers, Lord, ed. and trans. *Buddha's Teachings being the Sutta-Nipata or Discourse-Collection.* Harvard Oriental Series, vol. 37. Cambridge: Harvard University Press, 1932.

[6]   Padhana-sutta.

[7] *Collection of the Middle-Length Sayings (Majjhima-Nikaya).* Translated by I. B. Horner. 3 vols. London: Luzac and Co., 1959.

Davids, T. W. R., trans. *Buddhist Birth Stories or Jataka Tales.* London: Trubner and Co., 1880.

[8]   Introduction to the Jataka.

Dialogues of the Buddha (Digha-Nikaya). Sacred Books of the Buddhist Series. Vol. 2 (1956), T. W. Rhys Davids, trans.; vol. 3 (1966), vol. 4 (1965), T. W. Rhys Davids and C. A. F. Rhys Davids, trans. London: Luzac and Co.

[9]   Tevijja Sutta.

[10]   Lakkhana Suttanta.

[11]   Mahasatipatthana Suttanta.

[12]   Pottapada Sutta.

[13]   Samanna-phala Sutta.

[14]   Maha-Govinda Suttanta.

[15]   Kevaddha Sutta.

[16]   Atanatiya Suttanta.

[17]   Sigalovada Suttanta.

[18]   Kutadanta Sutta.

Bibliography

[19]   Cakkavatti-Sihanada Suttanta.

[20]   Agganna Suttanta.

[21]   Maha-Sudassana Suttanta.

Hamilton, Clarence H. *Buddhism*. New York: The Bobbs-Merrill Co., 1952.

[22]   Dhammapada.

[23] *Jataka, The*. Translated under the editorship of E. B. Cowell. 6 vols. and index. Cambridge, 1895–1913.

[24] *Kalama Sutta*. Translated by Soma Thera. The Wheel Publication No. 8. Kandy: Buddhist Publication Society, 1963.

[25] Khantipalo, Bhikkhu. *Patimokkha*. Bangkok: Social Science Association Press of Thailand, 1966.

[26] *Minor Readings (Khuddakapatha)*. Translated by Bhikkhu Nyanamoli. London: Luzac and Co., 1960.

[27] *Questions of King Milinda*. Translated by T. W. Rhys Davids. Part 1 and 2. Unabridged and unaltered republication of vol. 35 (1890) and vol. 36 (1894) of *The Sacred Books of the East*. New York: Dover Publications, 1963.

[28] Thomas, Edward Joseph. *Jataka Tales*. Cambridge: at the University Press, 1916.

[29] ———. *Buddhist Scriptures*. London: John Murray, 1913.

Vinaya Texts. The Sacred Books of the East. Vol. 4 and vol. 5, T. W. Rhys Davids and Hermann Oldenberg, trans. New York: Charles Scribner's Sons, 1899.

[30]   Mahavagga, vol. 4.

[31]   Cullavagga, vol. 4 and vol. 5.

Warren, Henry Clarke, trans. *Buddhism in Translations*. (1896) Reprint. New York: Atheneum, 1963.

[32]   Introduction to the Jataka.

[33]   Majjhima-Nikaya.

[34]   Milindapanha.

[35]   Visuddhi-Magga.

Bibliography

[36]   Samyutta-Nikaya.

[37]   Abhidhamnattha-Sangaha.

[38]   Khuddhaka-Nikaya, Udana.

B. General

[39] Adikaram, E. W. *Early History of Buddhism in Ceylon.* Colombo, Ceylon: M. D. Gunasena and Co., 1946.

[40] *Anthropological Studies in Theravada Buddhism.* Cultural Report Series No. 13. New Haven: Yale University Southeast Asia Studies, 1966.

[41] Bapat, Purushottam Vishvanath. *2500 Years of Buddhism.* Delhi: Ministry of Information and Broadcasting, Government of India, 1959.

[42] Bellah, Robert N. "Reflections on the Protestant Ethic Analogy in Asia." In *Journal of Social Issues* 19 (1963): 52–60.

[43] _____. *Religion and Progress in Modern Asia.* New York: Free Press, 1965.

[44] Benz, Ernst. *Buddhism or Communism: Which Holds the Future of Asia?* Translated by Richard and Clara Winston. New York: Doubleday and Co., Anchor Books, 1966.

[45] Berval, Rene de, ed. *Présence du Bouddhisme.* Saigon: France-Asie, 1959.

[46] Bouquet, A. C. *Comparative Religion.* New and rev. ed. London: Cassell, 1961.

[47] Brewster, E. H. *The Life of Gotama–the Buddha.* New York: E. P. Dutton and Co., 1926.

[48] Coèdes, G. *The Indianized States of Southeast Asia.* Edited by Walter F. Vella. Translated by Susan Brown Cowing. Honolulu: East-West Center Press, 1968.

[49] Conze, Edward. *Buddhism: Its Essence and Development.* New York: Harper, 1959.

[50] _____. *Buddhist Meditation.* London: G. Allen and Unwin, 1956.

[51] Dutt, Sukumar. *Buddhism in East Asia.* Delhi: Council for Cultural Relations, Caxton Press, 1966.

Bibliography

[52] _____. *The Buddha and Five After-centuries*. London: Luzac and Co., 1957.

[53] Eliot, Sir Charles. *Hinduism and Buddhism*. London: E. Arnold and Co., 1921.

[54] Finot, Louis. "Outlines of the History of Buddhism in Indo-China." In *Buddhistic Studies*, edited by B. C. Law, pp. 749–67. Calcutta: Thacker, Spink and Co., 1931.

[55] Gard, Richard A. *Buddhism*. New York: G. Braziller, 1961.

[56] Geiger, Wilhelm, trans. *The Mahāvaṃsa or The Great Chronicle of Ceylon*. Colombo, Ceylon: Ceylon Government, Information Department, 1960.

[57] Gokhale, Balkrishna Govind. *Buddhism and Asoka*. Baroda, India: Padmaja Publications, 1948.

[58] _____. "Theravada View of History." In *American Oriental Society Journal* 85 (1965):354–60.

[59] Hall, D. G. E. *A History of South-East Asia*. 3rd ed. New York: St. Martin's Press, 1968.

[60] Heine-Geldern, R. *Conceptions of State and Kingship in Southeast Asia*. Southeast Asia Program Data Paper no. 18. Ithaca: Cornell University, 1956.

[61] Kitagawa, Joseph M. "Buddhism and Asian Politics." In *Asian Survey* 2 (1962):1–11.

[62] Landon, Kenneth. *Southeast Asia: Crossroads of Religion*. Chicago: University of Chicago Press, 1949.

[63] Law, Bimala Churn. *The Buddhist Conception of Spirits*. 2d rev. ed. London: Luzac and Co., 1936.

[64] Le May, Reginald. *An Asian Arcady: The Land and Peoples of Northern Siam*. Cambridge: W. Heffer and Sons, 1926.

[65] _____. *The Culture of Southeast Asia*. London: George Allen and Unwin, 1964.

[66] Lévy, Paul. *Buddhism: A 'Mystery Religion'?* University of London: The Athlone Press, 1957.

[67] Myrdal, Gunnar. *Asian Drama*. 3 vols. New York: Pantheon, 1969.

[68] Niehoff, Arthur. "Theravada Buddhism: A Vehicle for Technical Change." In *Human Organization* 23 (1964).

[69] Nyanaponika, Thera. *The Power of Mindfulness.* The Wheel Publication no. 121/122. Kandy: The Buddhist Publication Society, 1968.

[70] Nyanasatta, Thera C. *Basic Tenets of Buddhism.* Rajagiriya, Ceylon: Ananda Semage, 1957.

[71] Pande, G. C. *Studies in the Origins of Buddhism.* Allahabad: Department of Ancient History, Culture and Archeology, University of Allahabad, 1957.

[72] Perera, H. R. *Buddhism in Ceylon.* The Wheel Publication no. 100. Kandy: The Buddhist Publication Society, 1966.

[73] Rahula, Walpola. *History of Buddhism in Ceylon.* Colombo, Ceylon: M. D. Gunasena and Co., 1956.

[74] _____. *What the Buddha Taught.* Bedford, England: The Gordon Fraser Gallery Limited, 1959.

[75] Rajadhon, Phya Anuman. "The Khwan and Its Ceremonies." In *Journal of Siam Society* 50 (1962):121.

[76] Schecter, Jerrold. *The New Face of the Buddha.* New York: Coward-McCann, 1967.

[77] Smith, Harvey H., et al. *Area Handbook for South Vietnam.* Washington, D.C.: The American University, 1967.

[78] Thomas, Edward Joseph. *The Life of Buddha.* 3d rev. ed. London: Routledge and Kegan Paul, 1949.

[79] Weber, Max. *The Sociology of Religion.* Boston: Beacon Press, 1963.

C. Burma

[80] Aung, Maung Htin. *Folk Elements in Burmese Buddhism.* London: Oxford University Press, 1962.

[81] Brohm, John Frank. "Buddhism and Animism in a Burmese Village." In *Journal of Asia Studies* 22 (1963):155–67.

[82] _____. "Burmese Religion and the Burmese Religious Revival." Ph.D. dissertation, Cornell University, 1957.

Bibliography

[83] Fielding-Hall, H. *The Soul of a People.* London: Macmillan and Co. Ltd., 1909.

[84] Hobbs, Cecil. "The Burmese Family: An Inquiry into its History, Customs and Traditions." Washington, D.C., n.p., 1952.

[85] King, Winston Lee. *A Thousand Lives Away.* Cambridge: Harvard University Press, 1965.

[86] _____. *In the Hope of Nibbana.* La Salle, Ill.: Open Court, 1964.

[87] Ling, T. "Social Dimension of Theravada Buddhism in Burma." In *Hibbert Journal* 60 (1962):314–22.

[88] Maung, Mya. "Cultural Value and Economic Change in Burma." In *Asian Survey* 4 (1964):757–64.

[89] Nash, Manning. "Buddhist Revitalization in the Nation State — The Burmese Experience." In *Religion and Change in Contemporary Asia*, edited by Robert F. Spencer. Minneapolis: University of Minnesota Press, 1971.

[90] _____. "Burmese Buddhism in Everyday Life." In *American Anthropologist* 65 (1963):285–95.

[91] _____. *The Golden Road to Modernity.* New York: John Wiley and Sons, 1965.

[92] Pannasami. *The History of the Buddha's Religion (Sāsanavaṃsa).* Translated by B. C. Law. London: Luzac and Co., 1952.

[93] Paw U, Richard. "The Buddhist Priesthood in Burmese Society." Master's thesis, Columbia University, 1948.

[94] Pe Maung Tin and Luce, G. H., trans. *The Glass Palace Chronicles of the Kings of Burma.* Rangoon: Rangoon University Press, 1960.

[95] Pfanner, David E. "Rice and Religion in a Burmese Village." Ph.D. dissertation, Cornell University, 1962.

[96] Pfanner, David E., and Ingersoll, Jasper. "Theravada Buddhism and Village Economic Behavior: A Burmese and Thai Comparison." In *Journal of Asian Studies* 21 (1962):341–61.

Bibliography

[97] Ray, Nihar-Ranjan. *An Introduction to the Study of Theravada Buddhism in Burma.* Calcutta: University of Calcutta, 1946.

[98] Sarkisyanz, Emanuel. *Buddhist Backgrounds of the Burmese Revolution.* The Hague: M. Nijhoff, 1965.

[99] Slater, Robert Lawson. *Paradox and Nirvana.* Chicago: University of Chicago Press, 1951.

[100] Smith, Donald Eugene. *Religion and Politics in Burma.* Princeton: Princeton University Press, 1965.

[101] Spiro, M. E. "Buddhism and Economic Action in Burma." In *American Anthropology* 68 (1966):1163–73.

[102] _____. *Buddhism and Society.* New York: Harper & Row, 1970.

[103] _____. *Burmese Supernaturalism.* Englewood Cliffs, N.J.: Prentice Hall, 1967.

[104] Temple, Sir. R. C. *The Thirty-seven Nats.* London: W. Griggs, 1906.

[105] Thet, U Kyaw. "Continuity in Burma." In *Perspective of Burma, Atlantic Monthly Supplement,* 1958, p. 23.

[106] Tinker, Hugh. *The Union of Burma.* London: Oxford University Press, 1967.

[107] Trager, Frank N. "Reflections on Buddhism and the Social Order in Southern Asia." In *Burma Research Society* 1 (1961): 529–43.

[108] Von der Mehden, Fred R. *Religion and Nationalism in Southeast Asia.* Madison: University of Wisconsin Press, 1963.

D. Cambodia

[109] Berval, Rene de, ed. *Présence du Cambodge.* Saigon: France-Asie, 1955.

[110] *Centers of Buddhist Studies in Cambodia.* Phnom Penh: Buddhist Institute, 1963.

[111] Chau Seng. *L'organization buddhique au Cambodge.* Phnom Penh: Université buddhique Preah Sihanouk Raj, 1962.

Bibliography

[112] Chou Ta-Kuan. *Notes on the Customs of Cambodia.* Translated by J. Gilman D'Arcy Paul. Bangkok: Social Science Association Press, 1967.

[113] Dhammarama, P. S. *Initiation pratique au Buddhisme.* Phnom Penh: Université buddhique Preah Sihanouk Raj, 1962.

[114] Leclère, Adhèmard. *Le bouddhisme au Cambodge.* Paris: E. Leroux, 1899.

[115] *Les paroles de Samdech Preah N. Sihanouk.* Phnom Penh: Ministry of Information, 1965–66.

[116] Porée-Maspéro, E. *Cérémonies des douze mois.* Phnom Penh: Commission on the Mores and Customs of Cambodia, n.d.

[117] Porée-Maspéro, M. "Cérémonies privées des Cambodgiens." In *Éditions de l'institut Bouddhique.* Phnom Penh, 1958.

[118] Sihanouk, Norodom. *Notre socialisme Buddhique.* Kambuja no. 8, November 15, 1965. Phnom Penh: Le Ministere de l'information.

[119] Steinberg, David J. *Cambodia: Its People, Its Society, Its Culture.* New Haven: HRAF Press, 1959.

E. Laos

[120] Abhay, Thao Nhouy. "Buddhism in Laos." In *Kingdom of Laos,* edited by Rene de Berval. Translated by Mrs. Teissier. Saigon: France-Asie, 1959, p. 243.

[121] Halpern, Joel M. *Government, Politics and Social Structure in Laos.* Monograph No. 4. New Haven: Yale University, Southeast Asia Studies, 1964.

[122] Lebar, Frank M., and Suddard, Adrienne. *Laos: Its People, Its Society, Its Culture.* New Haven: HRAF Press, 1960.

[123] Lévy, Paul. "Le traces de l'introduction du bouddhisme á Luang Prabang." *Bulletin de l'école française De'extrême-Orient,* edited by George Coèdes. XL, p. 411. Hanoi.

Bibliography

[124] Phouvong Phimmasone. "The Buddhist Institute and Religious Teaching." In *Kingdom of Laos*, edited by Rene de Berval. Translated by Mrs. Teissier. Saigon: France-Asie, 1959, p. 443.

F. Thailand

[125] *Acts on the Administration of the Buddhist Order of Sangha*. Bangkok: Mahamakuta Educational Council, 1963.

[126] *Annual Report of Religion Activities for 1965*. Bangkok: Department of Religious Affairs, 1965.

[127] Ayal, Eliezer B. "Value Systems and Economic Development in Japan and Thailand." In *Journal of Social Issues* 19 (1963):35–51.

[128] Blanchard, Wendell. *Thailand: Its People, Its Society, Its Culture*. New Haven: HRAF Press, 1958.

[129] Bodhiramsi. *Cāmadevīvaṃsa*. In "Documents sur l'histoire politique et religieuse du Laos Occidental," *Bulletin de l'école française De'extrême-Orient*, edited and translated by George Coèdes. Hanoi.

[130] *Book of Recitations for the Order of Bhikkhus of Thailand, A*. Bangkok: Mahamakuta Educational Council, 1957.

[131] Buribhand, Luang Boribal. *The History of Buddhism in Thailand*. Translated by Dr. Luang Suriyabongs. Bangkok: Chatra Press, 1955.

[132] Dhaninivat, Kromamun Bidyalabh. *A History of Buddhism in Siam*. Bangkok: Prachandra Press, 1959. Reprint, 1960.

[133] _____. *Monarchical Protection of the Buddhist Church in Siam*. Bangkok: World Fellowship of Buddhism, 1964.

[134] *General Information*. Mahachulalongkornrajavidyalaya University. Bangkok: Karnsasana Press, 1967.

[135] Hanks, L. M. "Merit and Power in the Thai Social Order." In *American Anthropology* 64 (1962):1247–61.

[136] Ingersoll, Jasper. "Fatalism in Village Thailand." In *Anthropology Quarterly* 39 (1966):200–250.

Bibliography

[137] Ishii, Yoneo. "Church and State in Thailand." In *Asian Survey* 2 (1962): 1–11.

[138] Khantipalo, Bhikkhu. *What Is Buddhism.* Bangkok: Social Science Association Press of Thailand, 1965.

[139] Kirsch, A. Thomas. "Phu Thai Religious Syncretism: A Case Study of Thai Religion and Society." Ph.D. dissertation, Harvard University, 1967.

[140] Klausner, William J. "Popular Buddhism in Northeast Thailand." In *Cross-Cultural Understanding,* edited by F. S. C. Northrup and Helen H. Livingston. New York: Harper & Row, 1964.

[141] Kusalasaya, Karuna. *Buddhism in Thailand.* Kandy: Buddhist Publication Society, 1965.

[142] Piker, Steven. "The Relationship of Belief Systems to Behavior in Rural Thai Society." In *Asian Survey* 8 (1968): 384–99.

[143] Rajadhon, Phya Anuman. *Life and Ritual in Old Siam.* New Haven: HRAF Press, 1961.

[144] Ratanapanna. *Jinakālamālinī.* In "Documents sur l'histoire politique et religieuse du Laos Occidental," *Bulletin de l'école française De'extrême-Orient,* edited and translated by George Coèdes. Hanoi.

[145] Suriyabongs, Dr. Luang. *Buddhism in the Light of Modern Scientific Ideas.* Bangkok: Mahamakut Academy, 1960.

[146] Tambiah, S. J. "The Ideology of Merit and the Social Correlates of Buddhism in a Thai Village." In *Dialectic in Practical Religion,* edited by E. R. Leach. London: Cambridge University Press, 1968.

[147] Textor, Robert B. "An Inventory of Non-Buddhist Supernatural Objects in a Central Thai Village." Ph.D. dissertation, Cornell University, 1960.

[148] *Thai Sangha, The.* Department of Religious Affairs. Bangkok: Karnsasana Press, 1967.

[149] *Thailand Year Book.* Bangkok: Temple Publicity Services, 1968.

Bibliography

[150] Thanim Laohawilai. *A Summary of the Solutions of the Six General Conferences of the World Fellowship of Buddhists*. Bangkok: World Fellowship of Buddhism, 1964.

[151] *U. S. Congressional Record*. 91st Congress, First Session, 1969, vol. 115, no. 36.

[152] Wachirayan, Warorat (Prince Vajiranana). *Right Is Right*. Bangkok: Bangkok Daily Mail, 1918.

[153] _____. *The Buddhist Attitude towards National Defence and Administration*. n.p., 1916.

[154] Wells, Kenneth Elmer. *Thai Buddhism*. Bangkok: Christian Bookstore, 1960.

[155] Wells, Margaret. *Guide to Chiengmai*. Bangkok: Christian Bookstore, 1967.

Index

Index

Index

Nu, U, 1, 78, 106

Offerings (*dakkhina*), the five;
see Gifts (*dana*), the five
Ordination, 49–52, 88–93, 142,
148

Pali-language, study of, 95, 123
Paritta (verse of protection):
chanted by the monk, 117,
137, 143; pronounced by the
Buddha, 42–45
Patimokkha, 50–52, 79, 93, 100,
104, 111
Perfections, the ten, 14, 18
Phii; see Spirits, Phii
Preah Sihanouk Raj Buddhist
University, 97–98, 127
Precepts, the: of the laity, 57–
59, 61, 63–64, 85, 111, 132,
139–40, 144; of the monk,
50, 85, 92–93, 144

Rainy Season (Vassa) Retreat,
52–53, 74, 88, 90, 113, 142,
144–45, 153
Raptures; see Absorptions
Rebirth, 27, 29, 37–38, 61, 86
Religious Affairs, Department
of, 101, 103, 105, 121, 123
Renunciation, the Great, 17, 92

Sakka (king of the gods), 14,
39, 135, 167 n. 26, 173 n. 26;
see also Gods (*deva*)
Sangha; see Bhikkhu-Sangha
Sangharaja (Supreme Patriarch), 78, 80, 100–102,
Shwegyin Order, 107–8, 110
Sihanouk, Norodom, 105,
126–27

Spirits: and the Buddha, 17,
39; the Buddha's power
over, 42–43, 67; exorcising
of, by Bhikkhu, 116–17,
140; festivals and, 142–46;
hungry ghosts (*peta*), 39–
41, 45–46, 60; the layman's
concern with, 134–38, 140,
181 n. 9; Nat, 91–92, 135–
38, 145, 181 n. 9; Phii, 138;
propitiated during ordination, 90–92; protection
against evil, 89–90, 175 n. 7;
royal decree concerning worship of, 77; see also Sukhwan
Sudhamma Order, 107–8, 110
Sukhwan, 91, 138, 140–41,
144–45

Theravada, definition of,
165 n. 1
Threefold Refuge (*ti-sarana*),
11, 49, 110–11
Three Jewels, the (*ti-ratana*),
42, 77, 92
Tipiṭaka, 12, 69, 71, 163–64

Uposatha, 52, 56, 59, 111–12,
124, 130–31, 139–40,
143–45

Vesakha festival, 104, 142–44
Vessantara, 14, 19, 63,
172 n. 59
Vipassana (insight), 33,
169 n. 28

Wheel of Becoming, 29–30
Wealth, economic, 57, 59–63,
147–49, 156–57
Worlds (*loka*), The, 38–41

F